Humanism and Imagination

HUMANISM

AND

IMAGINATION

By

G. R. Elliott

KENNIKAT PRESS, INC./PORT WASHINGTON, N. Y.

To

MY STUDENTS

in the University of Wisconsin,
Bowdoin College, and Amherst College
with such an affectionate gratefulness
as they are too modest to understand

Preface

MOST OF THE CHAPTERS IN THIS VOLUME HAVE APPEARED
in periodical form, but they have been considerably
altered, often extended, for the present publication. Their
present arrangement, which does not at all follow the order
of composition, took shape in my mind gradually while
they were being written. In Part Two there is a shift of
method and emphasis, for Emerson, the central figure in
Part Two, needs to be viewed in a context quite other than
that provided for Babbitt and More in Part One. The extraordinary gulf between the Emersonian gospel and the
"humanism" of those two powerful critics (the extremeness
of the difference comes out by contrast when we think of
the parallel but equable transition from Wordsworth to
Matthew Arnold) is due to a harmful extremism in the action of the American mind. It can be overcome, I believe,
only by the development of a more historic, dramatic, and
symbolical mode of imagination than we have exercised
hitherto. That belief lends, I hope, a certain underlying
unity to this book as a whole.

The symbolical, as just suggested, is associated throughout the volume with the dramatic and the historic, not with
the abstruse. (The reader is referred to the entries under

"Substance" and "Symbol" in the Index.) The words symbol, image, and myth need to be divested of the air of unreality which they have derived from transcendental theorizing, including Platonism at its worst. Particular things do not of necessity appear less real when regarded as symbolic. Individuality is enhanced, not depreciated, by true symbolism. A human person must be seen as more real *in and for himself* proportionally as he images or symbolizes something greater than himself. When the imagination has not a firm grip of that fact, it is immature, or diseased, or both.

Much of the material here used was first printed in *The American Review* and its predecessor *The Bookman*, owned and edited by Seward Collins, to whom I am very grateful. My thanks are also due to the following journals: *The Virginia Quarterly Review*, *The Saturday Review of Literature*, *The Forum*, *The New England Quarterly*, *The Bowdoin Alumnus*, *The University of Toronto Quarterly*, *The Examiner*, and *Religion in Life*.

G. R. E.

Amherst, Massachusetts
June, 1938

Contents

PART ONE

1.

The Divergence of Humanism
and the Spirit of Poetry

POETRY AND ACADEMIC CRITICISM, THOUGH NEVER BOSOM friends, have often approached each other. Today they are very far apart, especially in America. Our literary scholars have for many years, and for many good reasons, devoted themselves largely to what is called "literary science," particularly historical research. This fact (in addition to its pedagogic results, which I am to deal with later in a book on education and poetry) has had a pronounced effect upon the most substantial critical movement of the present time, academic humanism. I term it "academic" for two reasons: first, because of its claim that, unlike other current humanisms, it belongs in a tradition coming down from the Athenian grove; secondly, because its immediate roots are in vigorous and rigorous scholarship. Its leaders in France and America have been extraordinary in scholarly equipment, in the range and accuracy of their historico-philosophic knowledge of letters. These humanists are the heirs of an unprecedented era of research, albeit they have sharply criticized its purposes. Deprecating "literary science," they have brought literary scholarship into the service of moral principles. But, so far, they have not been much interested in poetry. They have fulfilled Matthew Arnold's injunction to rise above mere "scientific curiosity," but they have sought to diffuse light rather than the "sweet-

ness and light" which he advocated. In re-establishing moral
ideas they have neglected the spirit of poetry. Meanwhile
this spirit, I mean the spirit of art and imaginative literature,
has increasingly neglected moral ideas, devoting itself to
peripheral notions that are soon "gone with the wind." Today we have a popular literature that is exuberantly non-
moral—appetitive, technicolored, moving-picturesque—and,
over against it, a critical humanism that is devoted impersonally and intellectually to ethical truth. The gap that
there always is between poetry and academic criticism is
today a gulf.

One feels that situation keenly in pondering the total
work of the distinguished critic who has recently been
taken from us, Paul Elmer More. His love of art and imaginative literature was warm but constricted. His books are
profound in morals and philosophy but not in poetry—
poetry as a way of looking at life. Hence his touch upon
the chief English poets, notably Shakespeare and Milton, is
inadequate; his attitude towards them is on the whole
remarkably incomprehensive. His treatment of the Romantic and naturistic writers has many superb insights, but
generally it is too narrow and rigid. Mr. More himself was
well aware of the aloofness of his criticism from the immediate motives of art. But like his friend Irving Babbitt,
and considerably under his influence, he was convinced
that a real revival of humanism demanded an unswerving
insistence upon fundamental moral laws. These, he believed,
must be presented to the modern mind with cutting edges;
the critic must not run the risk of dulling them with poeti-
cal considerations. Certainly that risk is always with us, and
certainly More avoided it himself and reduced it for others.
But he did not avoid the opposite danger, that of overriding
the poetic view of life with the historico-moral view, a

danger inherent in the new humanism because of its basis in historical research. When the literary scientist or the sheer moralist is unjust to poetry, no great harm is done since their lack of jurisdiction is obvious. But the danger is acute in the case of such a critic as More, for he speaks with authority. More has a real and fine feeling for poetry; but his conception of poetry, of its nature and function in the universe, is not full and just. His work as a whole seems to deny, and certainly blurs, the fact that poetry is an entirely distinct—not, of course, independent—way of looking at life.

I am obviously here using the word "poetry" in a very inclusive sense; one which, however, is familiar to us all. Coleridge proposed, in the interests of critical nomenclature, that the wider sense should be denoted by the word "poesy"; but his better instincts, no doubt, kept him from pressing the point. For "poesy," even if it could be rescued from its modern connotation of mere prettiness, would remain heavily tethered to the realm of art and letters; and there is a deep naturalness in our refusal to confine "poetry" to that realm. Naturally and normally we speak of the poetry of business, of history, of architecture, of trees, of religion, of Emerson's ideas, of Washington's life, of life itself. Poetry, in its most obvious and popular meaning, is a relief from conscience. In its higher modes it is an enlargement of conscience; but here, too, there is relief. Poetry is always relief from purely moral concentrations. Without such concentrations, life would soften and dissolve away; but without poetry, it would not be worth preserving. Human history looked at from the merely moral standpoint, supposing this to be possible, is not just a failure: it is an uninteresting, a very dull failure; it palls upon our spirits. But ever, "Some shape of beauty moves away the pall. . . ."

The word "shape" is significant. In that twelfth line of his proem to *Endymion* Keats subtly if unconsciously develops and clarifies the truth of his opening verses:

> A thing of beauty is a joy for ever:
> Its loveliness increases; it will never
> Pass into nothingness. . . .

This poet is keenly aware that every "thing" of beauty is transitory in so far as it is an object visible to our physical eyes; but he knows that it is not transitory in so far as it is a true "shape" of beauty. Such shapes indeed remain forever, according to poetic and religious faith. Religion, by itself, can exclaim with sublime indiscrimination that "the things which are seen are temporal but the things which are not seen are eternal." But religion joined with poetry knows that a "shape of beauty" is at once seen and unseen, mysteriously but really: it cannot "pass into nothingness." Intimations of that truth are with us every day. Our memory is stored with living forms of things that have passed away, that have died out of the world or out of the world of our present experience: a brook loved in childhood, a good person who swayed us in youth, a splendid action that we witnessed yesterday. And we perceive, no matter how vaguely, that there is something *essential* in these loved and lasting forms. Accordingly those forms become "essences" in the second unfolding of Keats's thought in his great proem. In the twelfth line he speaks of "some shape of beauty"; further on, after another dozen lines, the poet is driven and inspired to speak of "essences." (Those two divisions of twelve lines each are not mere mathematic chance: they indicate the essential symmetry of the poet's mood here.) His thought is now that "these essences," after moving the pall from our dark spirits, persist "till they become a cheering light unto our souls": they become "bound to us so fast," so involved in our essential being, that "they alway must be with us, or we die." We live, said Arnold, very largely upon our "unconscious poetry." He meant, or ought to have meant, that we feed unawares upon the something of eternal life mediated to us through the poetry in our lives; through "the pleasure which there is in life itself," as Wordsworth put it—a "pleasurable feeling of blind love" for those shapes which, partaking at once of the seen and the unseen, pass vitally into our very being.

To be sure, we are apt to deny that our "unconscious poetry" has in it anything of eternal value when, as we say, we "stop to think," when we "use our reason." But the phrase "stop to think" in this context is a giveaway. It means, bluntly, that we stop living. Precisely it means that we check the full and normal process of life by isolating and employing one of the instruments of life, our "reason" —but not our Reason, our *Vernunft*, that complete action of the mind which great poetic thinkers have and which, in moments, all of us may experience; not that, but just our faculty for commonsensible ratiocination, a very useful faculty but incapable of apprehending the fundamental facts of religion or poetry. That sentence, I know, is "a mouthful." But, as one fire burns out another's burning, I am justified in employing pedantry against the pedantry of rationalism. I have dealt with the thing after a more human fashion in a later chapter on "Life Dramatic."

Of course our "reason" helps to keep us from being carried away by false or sentimental imagery. But it deceives us when it makes us feel that poetic form must be, more or less, insubstantial. Doubtless there is a true antithesis between "form" and "matter," but not between "form" and "substance" when substance is seen as spiritual. St. Paul sees it thus when, in expounding the Christian doctrine of immortality, he speaks of the "spiritual body." The primitive notion of disembodied spirits, though popularly maintained in the Christian era, is repugnant to the very genius of Christianity, which knows that a soul has, or rather is, a form more real than its fleshly body. To an unprecedented degree Christianity has endowed poets with what may be called a *personal* sense of "the things which are not seen." This is most striking in the case of those writers of the past four centuries whose work has been for the most part pagan; above all, Shakespeare. Beneath the vivid pagan surface of his writings one catches often a keen personal sense, fostered by Christianity (far more than by Platonism), for divinely human realities. But in him that sense is not so sure and pervasive as it is in his elder contemporary, the Christian poet, Edmund Spenser. I term him "the Christian poet" because far too much has been made of his Platonism and far too little of his Christianity, in which alone his Platonism lived and moved and had its being. The peculiar greatness of this poet is due to his strong and constant perception of the substantiality of transcendent forms, together with his rich endowment in the faculty that embodies them in poetry, namely the mythological imagination.

Here I wish to dwell a little on Spenser. Modern criticism has emphasized his shortcomings to the utmost. Yet he remains a very great writer: the third at the least among the poets in our language, despite Arnold's shortsighted attempt to insert his friend Wordsworth into that position. Arnold's

obtuseness in regard to Spenser is typically modern; it is
characteristic particularly of the later nineteenth and earlier
twentieth centuries. It is due at bottom to a fading of belief
in the eternal meaning of poetry. Arnold urged us to live
by poetry rather than religion but, as I have hinted above,
one doubts the depth, though not the graciousness, of his
religious faith in poetry. Spenser pre-eminently had that
faith; had it all the more and all the better because he did
not confuse belief in poetry with belief in religion or
imagine that either could take the place of the other. For
him the Christian religion, standing clearly on a height
above poetry, sends down into it a sublime invigoration, as
the old hermit "heavenly Contemplation" sends down the
Red Cross Knight from "the highest Mount" to put his
new "grace" into his worldly labors. When Spenser writes
in his *Hymne in Honour of Beautie,* "For soule is form and
doth the body make," he is not just echoing a Christian
Platonic tradition, he is uttering a living, personal conviction upon which is founded that magnificent and truthful
palace of art, *The Faerie Queene.*

Today Spenser can give us special help in disentangling
ourselves from what he would call a prime "Errour"
("Strangle her, els she sure will strangle thee"), the error of
supposing that poetic form is necessarily unreal.[1] And
Spenser's chief modern pupil, Keats, can give us the same
help if we read him humanely, not romantically in the
cheaper sense of this word. When Keats in his well-known
letter of October 25, 1818, speaks of "the mighty abstract
Idea of Beauty in all things" he does not mean that this Idea
is abstract in the sense of being in the least unreal. The context shows that it is abstract in comparison with "the chairs

[1] A new and fine understanding of Spenser appears in C. S. Lewis's
book, *The Allegory of Love,* London, 1936.

and sofa," with everyday things experienced from the
standpoint of everyday comfort and happiness. It is "abstract" and "sublime" because it is more real than those
things. For Keats, indeed, it is a Real Presence. It is that
substantial Form in which all true forms subsist. He goes
on to say that it provides his imagination with "shapes of
epic greatness." And that phrase brings us back to the
proem of *Endymion* with its shapes of beauty which are
immortal "essences"—

> An endless fountain of immortal drink,
> Pouring unto us from the heaven's brink.

For a certain type of romantic person that couplet is so
beautiful that it does not need to be true; for a certain type
of "humanist" it cannot be very true because it seems so
romantic. But in fact it has a beauty that is entirely true.
Incidentally it is accurate, for example in the word "unto."
That "fountain of immortal drink" cannot pour *into* us
unless, when it comes down *unto* us, we also come unto it:
the action of the human will is implied; as, dare I say, in the
sublime poem recorded by St. Matthew that begins, "Come
unto me." But what we need to perceive is the truth of the
whole image and movement of those two lines: they give us
a true vision of the seen and unseen universe in action as
beauty. That couplet is solid poetic fact.

Solid poetic fact. Below I have recounted how ill that
phrase of mine fared at the hands of the late Irving Babbitt
during our discussions. He could not be budged from his
contention that beauty cannot be a final criterion like goodness: the ultimate question in regard to either beauty or
truth must be, How good is it? This is undeniable, of
course, if the word "good" be taken in its ultimate mean-

ing. A great deal of confusion has been caused by the ambiguity of the final term in the triad "beauty, truth, and goodness." Surely "virtue" or "righteousness" would be better; "goodness" being reserved for the summum bonum, the ultimate and indivisible quality that comprises the virtuous, the beautiful, and the true. In common speech our tone, more than our diction, indicates our sharp awareness of the difference between a merely moral goodness and a complete goodness. When we remark of a man, "Oh, yes, he's very good but—," our tone can render further words superfluous. On the other hand, we can say of a rare person in a rare moment, "He is *good*," in a tone that means he exemplifies something of what religion calls "the *utter* goodness of God." This phrase recognizes the fact that goodness which is merely moral is not an ultimate criterion any more than truth or beauty is.

Arnold was thoroughly aware of that fact; he had a constant feeling for complete goodness, and it gave him greatness of tone. His value as a critic resides in his tone rather than his ideas. These have been perforated more and more by subsequent critics, but none of them has equaled him in largeness and fineness of tone. The reasonings involved in his doctrine of "perfection" are very vulnerable but his tone is right: his books are pervaded by a steady and yet flexible devotion to human perfection. His quality of firm flexibility has given him a special appeal to thoughtful Americans because it is a quality that the civilization of their country sorely needs. Arnold's possession of it is due in the main to his understanding of poetry, not so much its art as its way of looking at life: his humanism is at one with poetry. But, unfortunately, a main line of his logic prepared indirectly for the present divergence of poetry and humanism. Obsessed with the notion that the Anglo-Saxon race had attended sufficiently for the time being to the idea of duty, he preached beauty and truth ("sweetness and light") in a fashion that seemed to partition them off from morality. To be sure, as he increasingly sensed the *fin-de-siècle* moral decadence, he insisted roundly that "conduct is three fourths of life." But this picturesque dictum serves to establish the unfortunate partition which he had set up. He would better have urged that "conduct" in a far fuller sense than the merely moral, "conduct" as the procedure of the best human will in pursuit of virtue, truth, and beauty, is *four* fourths of life.

Arnold's treatment of the human will is shallow in comparison with that of his two chief successors, Babbitt and More. They saw that the will at its best is not partitionable; it is an entity. They were right and timely in urging that "the higher will," as they called it, is essentially the same in the realms of art and intellect as in the realm of morals: its presence or absence determines whether poetry, knowledge, or action shall be high or low. But they stressed overwhelmingly the moral aspect of the will, particularly its function in checking the appetites. The value of that emphasis should not be missed. Nevertheless the "higher will" is not valid as an entity operative in every department of life in so far as it is sheerly a will to righteousness. The Highest Will, the Good Will, the Will to Goodness, is at once righteous and true and beautiful. It cannot be one of these more than it is the others. It stresses here one of them and there another; but it employs with equal validity those three modes; and criticism is misleading when it says or implies the contrary. Poetry is no less distinctive in its standpoint than ethical philosophy or religion. Great poetry, such as Keats's proem, is in accord with virtue and truth while, and because, it pursues its own way. Hence it gives us what I have called solid *poetic* fact.

The facts of life range from vile to sublime, and great poetry ranges with them, seeing each in its proper place. Spenser, the so-called poet of beauty, is also the poet of ugliness. Recent writers who have devoted themselves to "the durtie ground," as Spenser spells it suggestively, have not explored it so effectually as he. They are propagandists for it. They have not viewed it proportionally; they have not achieved form: they are, in another phrase from Spenser, "full of great lumpes of flesh and gobbets raw." No doubt any raw stuff that is really actual, every fresh and sincere experience of life, brutal or divine, has its potential value for art. Always in the history of art and literature a new phase of Form is preceded by a busy digging of new raw materials. But these materials, though really actual, are not actually real. Our modern actualists, our diggers of raw materials, are commonly known as "realists" only because of our extraordinarily deficient sense of the reality of Form. The most damning feature of the situation is that many intelligent reviewers palliate formlessness, or cheap form, in a new poem or novel because they find in it what they regard as "reality" but which is mere actuality. Spenser, in spite of his occasional touches of actualism and propaganda, is a true realist. In *The Faerie Queene* he *informs* a thousand levels of life, from the "durtie ground" in the first canto to the "great goddesse Nature" in the last. As he proceeds we can watch him continually intensifying his patterns of evil while enlarging, above them, his Pattern of the Good; until at the close he has a vision of a "Nature" which is the nature of the Deity. "Nature" here is the poetic form of "that great Sabbaoth God" to whom the poet prays in his final and piercing verses.

Critics have all too glibly assumed that *The Faerie Queene*, if it had been completed according to the design sketched by the author in his letter to Raleigh, would have been hoplessly loose; but I shall not discuss that matter here. Certainly the poem as we have it, sadly lacking in wholeness of form, is in this respect inferior to *Othello* and *Paradise Lost*. Nevertheless Spenser excels his two chief successors in range of poetic vision; his range exceeds Shakespeare's vertically and Milton's horizontally; while, like them, he has that extraordinary capacity achieved by the Renaissance at its best for seeing each fact of life in its true poetic, and therefore in its true ethical, posture. In particular he is a master of the art of complementary episode—of creating related patterns that richly illuminate each other and suggest a scale of values in which each has its place: one "shape of beauty" points silently, as with a "magic hand of chance," to another shape below it or above it. In his canto on the House of Holiness, to take an obvious example, he makes no explicit allusion to its predecessor, the House of Pride, but he sets up in the reader's mind a tingling network of comparisons and contrasts. In our childhood the House of Holiness seems to us comparatively pale; we respond to the vivid pageantry of the House of Pride. But as the years go on, if we are constant readers of this poet, we come to see that his House of Holiness is one of the world's chief poetic creations. Not that the House of Pride fades for us—quite the contrary: we catch more and more its full significance and charm; and thus it serves more and more as foil for the greater significance and charm of the House of Holiness. This is no longer pale as it was for us in our early years; we see that its pageantry has a finer quality of vividness than that of the House of Pride. The whole canto moves, and moves with equal ease, on a higher and far more difficult level of beauty and of form.

"On a higher moral level," says the moralist bluntly. For poetry, however, that consideration is beside the point. If Spenser had not been able to build so superbly his House of Pride he could not have built so nobly his House of Holiness. A parallel fact in the moral sphere is that a man who is never tempted by pride cannot exercise the full humility of holiness. But for the poet, as such, the moral question is in abeyance. If Spenser's chief aim in the fourth canto of the first book of *The Faerie Queene* had been to show the sinfulness of pride he could not have written the canto. His chief aim was to draw out all his varied experience of pride and its concomitants into a full and fresh poetic pattern. He gives us pride's proper beauty, romantic, gorgeous, deadly; then he erects above it, in his tenth canto, a pattern of the simple, radiant, and life-giving beauty of holiness. Such is the way of great poetry. It is not great because it is moral; it is moral because it is great. It does not strive for higher moral levels; it attains these incidentally while striving for larger and more inclusive forms of experience. It is pervaded by the perception, extraordinarily keen in the case of Spenser, that brutal and evil shapes, no matter how vivid, indeed in the very quality of their vividness, are comparatively unreal, are subservient to the universal and substantial Pattern which no poet excepting God can comprehend.

> I faine to tell the things that I behold,
> But feel my wits to faile, and tongue to fold.

So exclaims Spenser when, towards the end of his life, he yearns for a nearer reflection of that Pattern in his great *Hymne of Heavenly Beautie.*

Even as I was brooding upon these things there came to my hands a small posthumous volume by Paul E. More, *Pages from an Oxford Diary*. I read it, absorbed: it touched me like a message from the beyond. For here the author attains an intenser glimpse of cosmic beauty than, I think, is to be found in any of his previous writings. After confronting a series of personal religious problems he declares, at the beginning of Section xxiii, "The final answer to my questioning was given in a vision of beauty one perfect day last summer." That is an extraordinary sentence to come from the pen of More. He proceeds to show how a lovely scene in the Severn Valley, as he meditated upon the long ages of evolution that had produced it, became for him a revelation of the divine "will and intelligence working out a design . . . through slowly yielding difficulties." He sees the mystery of evil ugliness subserving the beauty of the divine goodness. In other words this great critic towards the close of his life (like the poet Spenser in his *Hymne of Heavenly Beautie*) lifts his eyes and fixes them upon the cosmic Design in its sheer, substantial beauty. The moral battle of life, with which he had been so much preoccupied, retreats a little and is seen in perspective. Here More perceives, though he does not say so, the significant distinctiveness of the way of poetry.

Without that perception humanism cannot be fully human. With that perception, steadily and strongly cultivated, humanism can in time exert a renovating effect upon modern art and imaginative writing. The academic humanist should remain academic in the best sense of the word and cease to be so in a less desirable sense. He should in no way soften or compromise his tradition of ethical truth; but he should realize how unethical it is to blur the distinctiveness of the tradition of poetry. For life cannot be seen in its true ethic proportions without the aid of poetry's way of looking at life. Doubtless Arnold had that fact in mind when he asserted that poetry is "a criticism of life," though this phrase violates poetry's tone and method. Poetry is a proportioned vision of life; but the purer and higher it is, the less is it animated by any critical motive. Hence its witness to ethical truth is uniquely impartial; and the integrity of that witness must be cherished by humane criticism.

Recently I heard a Yankee carpenter condemn in the following words the work of a builder who had remade an old dwelling: "Th' sills" (i.e., the ground beams) "of thet house wa'n't true an' he ought t' hev trued 'em." The critic should strive continually to true the sills of his thought by studying the ground lines of poetry. Keeping distinct the poetic and the moral standpoints he should move from one to the other with a firm flexibility, which is not common today. Our popular book reviewers have now attained the suppleness of jellyfish, those alluring creatures that undulate and revolve in the crisscross currents off our New England shores. But a backboned flexibility, like that of the human body at its athletic best, is needed for humane criticism. Incidentally that word "humane" in its rich old denotation should gradually revive and overshadow, if not displace, the somewhat unhandsome adjective "humanistic" which academic humanists have perforce employed to mark their outlook off from that of humanitarianism. Certainly the word "humane" in the sense in which it applies to the jellyfish schools of current criticism does not apply to the poetry of Spenser, Shakespeare, and Milton. Yet one is not exactly happy in terming that poetry "humanistic"! It had better be called "humane" with the signification that the word had in the time of those poets. And modern humanism can become more humane in that sense by saturating itself

with the spirit and outlook which those great poets, despite
all their differences, exemplify in common.

Modern specialistic scholarship has divided Spenser,
Shakespeare, and Milton from each other. It has also divided
each of them into many pieces, the which are studied carefully in divers courses in our universities and colleges.
Time is now ripe for beginning to put the pieces together.
More largely speaking, we must strive to envisage the
poetry of the English Renaissance as a whole, with its three
chief poets representing three successive phases of it, three
aspects of its uniquely opulent and complete pattern. This
pattern begins nowadays to appear in something like its
true perspective. It was too recent to be comprehended by
students in the eighteenth and nineteenth centuries: partial
views held sway successively, neoclassic, romantic, naturalistic, and what not. In the years ahead, perhaps the most important single task for humane criticism is that of rescuing
the three leading poets in our language from those partial
views, the task of representing them in the full light of the
humane outlook that dominates their work. This task,
slow as it must be in accomplishment, will be in the end the
most effectual means of humanizing modern poetry. For
poetry is definitively affected only by poetry. In this sphere
"first in beauty" is always "first in might." Spenser, Shakespeare, and Milton, in countless indirect and hidden ways,
will continue, until they are surpassed, to exert the pre-
dominant influence upon their successors in the English
tongue. But their influence will be humane only in so far
as they are humanely read.

They cannot be rightly understood apart from catholic [2]

---

[2] I choose to spell this word in its present context with a small "c."
The use of capitals throughout this book, in the case of certain words, is
regularly irregular.

Christianity. It instituted and governed their humaneness. Of course many objections can be made to that statement. Above I have hinted how it applies to Spenser; elsewhere I have tried to suggest the way in which it applies to Milton and Shakespeare. Modern specialism has docketed Spenser as a romantic and Platonic visionary, Milton as a Puritan classicist, and Shakespeare as a glorious pagan. But far more significant than their dissimilarities is the quality they have in common, their catholic Christian humaneness. It comprises and dominates another quality which they share—very obvious in Shakespeare but no less important in Spenser and Milton—namely Renaissance naturalness, or naturalism.

This naturalism, more and more during the past two centuries, escaped from Christianity and allied itself with sentimental humanitarianism. A parallel and more or less causal phenomenon was the *poetic* decline of the Christian Church. Religion is (like nothing else) greater than poetry, but its long history has shown over and over again that religion (like everything else) is bound to crumble when it is poetically inadequate; that is, when its "poetry," in the inclusive meaning of this word exposed above, is too meagre or too cheap. One way of expressing the supremacy of Christianity is to say that it and it alone is, in its most catholic aspect, entirely adequate poetically. But just for that reason the narrowing and stiffening of the Christian imagination during the post-Reformation era, both in the Catholic and in the Protestant branches of the Church, was extraordinarily disastrous. Happily that era is now fast closing. And at the same time naturalism in its most rabid forms, speculative and literary, appears to be dissolving in its chemic mud. We must hope that the next two centuries will reverse the process of the past two: that the Christian

imagination in a modern and yet catholic mode will regain
its ascendancy over literature and art, and convert our comparatively unreal naturalism into a sound and vital naturalness. We must hope; but not too hopefully. For the very
fact that non-Christian naturalism is ridding itself of its
deadliest excrescences can give it a new lease of life; that
is, a new lease of death. Death, in the upshot, is what it
believes in. It does not believe in the Eternity which is at
once divine and human; and which is ultimately unbelievable without the Christian revelation (or, if you prefer,
manifestation) of that Eternity. Incidentally naturalism
cannot believe, though it may pretend to, that there is anything really eternal in poetry. For it is "too late," as Sir
Thomas Browne would say, to claim that poetry in its
highest reaches can be independent (as well as distinct)
from Christianity: such independence has been fully tried
and found wanting. Also it is "too late" to claim that adequate religious truth, let alone beauty, can be found outside
of Christianity: those purlieus have been thoroughly
searched and are found wanting. They have been searched
by non-Christian naturalists yearning for a firm ground of
faith. They have been searched by very spiritual thinkers.
They have been searched by the most comprehensive
skeptical intellect of our time, Paul E. More. It is of the
utmost significance that the far and wide journeyings of
such a critic brought him in the end to catholic Christianity.

   That is the direction in which criticism should now move
if impelled by its perennial effort to see life whole. And
that is the direction in which art and imaginative literature
will presently have to move if they are to deepen their
springs and become something more than fools of time,
providers of passing thrills; if they are to recapture that
serious social attention which is now pre-empted by the

social, natural, and practical sciences; if, in short, poetry is to become again social, natural, and "practical." Of course the naturalistic writers have been practical after a fashion. Though shallow and transient as artists and thinkers they have served, as propagandists, to expose the terrible ills of modern society. However, the kind of imagination which their books exemplify and foster is not the kind that promotes a real remedy for those ills since it does not find in the sufferers any real reality. But Christianity does. And the Christian imagination when it again pervades literature can shape the dark materials of naturalism in such a way as to move the social will, not just the spasmodic social sentiments, on behalf of wretched persons who are, as Spenser says and believes, "the images of God in earthly clay." So much by way of answer to the "practical" person who exclaims, "What has this poetry you're talking so much about to do with our great modern needs?" The answer is, "Everything." Poetry, which ceases to be itself when it tries to be practical, is in the long run the most practical power in the world. It affects our practices, insidiously and profoundly, for good and for ill; for good in so far as it has in it—implicitly, I mean, for I am not speaking of religious literature—the immortal, just, and catholic charity of Christ the Word.

My contention is therefore twofold regarding academic humanism. If it is to correct the divergence of poetry from moral truth, it must correct its own divergence from poetry; and, while maintaining its own proper bounds, it must co-operate with those religious thinkers who are developing a Christian outlook at once modern and catholic. Paul E. More in the final phase of his thought tended to submerge in religion the proper bounds of humanism; but this tendency, rectified as it is in a total view of his work, is not at all disastrous. Somewhat disastrous, however, was his venture into the inmost circles of the science of theology, as demonstrated with keen and charitable penetration in the writings of the Reverend W. N. Pittenger of the General Theological Seminary, New York. My own treatment of this matter, below, is meagre theologically, but true, I hope, to the standpoint of poetry. And that must be my answer to a humorous friend who, after reading some of the ensuing chapters, writes to me: "How about your *own* theology? Perhaps I would agree with it if I could make out what it is." Well, I myself have not made out exactly what it is. But obviously I do not have to do so in a book on "Humanism and Imagination." As its title indicates, this volume is not primarily concerned with the primary concern of life, religion. It is, however, much concerned with that which vitally affects every department of life, the imagination—imagination and the spirit of poetry. And this recurrent theme may lend some continuity of interest to a book devoid of that strictly logical unity which is so outstanding in the works of other academic humanists. With firm logic Irving Babbitt argued that modern persons should learn to be human again before trying to be saints. Paul E. More argued that our humanity must be infirm without the Catholic Christian Faith. They were both right, I believe. But I would add by way of footnote to those masters that the spirit of poetry, distinctively and humanely conceived, is a necessary aid to a faith and to a humanism that desire to be catholic.

2.

Irving Babbitt as I Knew Him

M^{Y FIRST SIGHT OF BABBITT WAS TWO DECADES AGO. I HAD} read his publications with mixed feelings, with admiration for his scholarship and force but with irritation at his roughshod treatment, as it seemed to me, of poetic imagination. Nor was that annoyance soothed away by a kind note which he had written to me upon an early essay of my own. I was a young professor of English literature in Bowdoin College and certainly words of commendation from Professor Babbitt were welcome; but he accompanied those words with other words urging that I should modify my point of view; and the proposed modification appeared to boil down to this, that I should adopt *his* point of view. This was not what he consciously intended to say; it was what I decided, upon reflection, that his note meant. I replied with critical sharpness and personal irritation. He wrote again, with a critical sharpness far surpassing mine, but with no personal irritation. That was irritating. I resolved to get a sight of this man who, like the Unmoved Mover of his master Aristotle, could cause an emotion which he did not feel or which, at least, he could fully repress. During my next visit to the Harvard Yard I joined the stream of students entering his classroom (having been informed that he was quite oblivious to foreign particles in that stream) and took a chair at the rear.

The man who presently entered the room and seated himself behind the desk was of big frame, slightly stooped.

The face was craggy, the jaw obtrusive, the voice vibrant, the gestures quick and angular. And certainly when he spoke he laid down the law; but not as though the law were his own. It belonged to humanity, so he made one feel; it had been enacted by the parliament of history and he was a clerk announcing it. He did so in tones full of its importance but empty of his own. I had known many professors who were modest because they were mild, and some who were not modest because they were professors. But Babbitt was neither mild nor officious. The moral laws were for him too clear, urgent, and fateful to permit of gentle circumspection in the enouncing of them; but also they were so transcendent as to belittle his office.

He spoke to the students as if they were on his own level. The fact that they were not was sufficiently apparent to most of them, but not to all. A certain youth, sitting reclined with half-closed eyes, folded arms, and supercilious smile, interrupted the lecturer with a drawling objection. My professorial nerves gave a sympathetic twitch: such a youngster ought to be told that the brilliance of his mind could be heightened by an erect and becoming posture of his body. But Babbitt, showing no irritation and scarcely any cognizance of the young man's physical presence, descended upon his notions like a courteous bombshell. In this classroom as in Europe a war was under way, but a warfare of ideas, hard, polite, impersonal. Freedom of speech was the rule, but the master's manner intimated that true freedom of speech required freedom from personalities. There was something aloof in the shooting glances with which he surveyed his class. Incessantly his eyes and hands dived into the untidy heap of books and papers on his desk. That heap was his ammunition dump. One watched fascinatedly while he extracted from its depths with inerrant dispatch the particular missile he wanted. He loaded his guns with citations; if you loaded yours with personal feelings, so much the worse for you. Piques and parades were negligible; personal inspirations were heavily discounted. To return his fire with any effect you had to let off an impersonal idea charged with solid fact.

But solid fact, for him, was apparently always moral fact; whereas I cherished the belief that there was such a thing as solid poetic fact. Was that belief merely a youthful illusion which a man who had passed his thirtieth birthday ought to leave behind him? Such was the question that forced itself upon me as I sat there silent. My answer was No, a loud internal No; which sounded there, however, like a rifle shot amid bursting shells. When the bombardment ceased, that is when the class hour ended, I advanced to the professor's desk and waited till a buzzing cluster of students had dispersed. Then I tackled him upon what seemed to me the least defensible assertion he had made during the hour. I forget now what it was, except that it had to do with poetic imagination. But I remember that presently I experienced the sensations of an outpost of soldiery who, on approaching a supposedly unguarded spot in the enemy's line, are greeted by a pretty nest of machine guns. An amicable parley ensued, however; and a friendship began.

But our meetings were not very frequent until the academic year 1927–28 which I spent on sabbatical leave in Cambridge, partly to be near the Harvard library, partly to be near Babbitt. Earlier I should doubtless have been afraid to expose myself to his fire at such close quarters for so considerable a period. But now I was middle-aged; my art of defense was better; and Babbitt, growing old, was less explosive than formerly. Not that his vigor showed any signs of diminution. He was as full of labors as ever, and much of his scanty leisure was devoted to strenuous walking combined with strenuous thinking. One who wished to talk with him extensively had to walk with him extensively; thus he economized his time, killing two birds with one stone. Often I felt like one bird killed with two stones: physically and mentally exhausted I would totter home after parting from him, wondering whether I should be able three or four days later to keep our appointment for what he termed, euphemistically, "another little walk together." Never have I been so exercised, in several senses of this word, as I was during those three seasons, autumn, winter and spring, in and about flat Cambridge. The sequel, the fourth season, was the summer of 1931 when I rented a vacation cottage not far from his among New Hampshire hills.

That was his last season of unbroken health. On an afternoon of July two years later his body lay silent in the chancel of the new Harvard chapel. That final scene was strange, hard to believe; though all of its externals were congruous enough. The service was austerely plain. Passages of excellent moral scripture, Christian and non-Christian, were recited from the high reading-desk, which closed a vista of white walls made whiter by the light of day. But the casket, beneath the desk, was covered with a crimson pall; and the sentences that were uttered above it had in them frequent words of rich and deep color. There came to me and doubtless to others who were present a mysterious, overmastering sense of a glow of life in white light. . . . Presently I remembered hearing Babbitt humorously excuse himself for seldom attending the sermons delivered in this very chapel: they were not such, he had said, as to enable him with clear conscience to desert what-

ever piece of work he had on hand at the time. Then, instead of that place, which seemed to me a glorified lecture-
hall rather than a church, I saw again in memory Babbitt's
own lecture room with himself at the desk. I began to recall
him vividly in all the scenes wherein I had known him in
life.

Walking on the hillsides of southern New Hampshire he
would sometimes pause to call my attention to a scene that
he loved. Not that he would *say* he loved it: the first person
singular of the verb "love" was regularly omitted from his
oral declensions. Whether and to what extent the words "I
love" took form in his mind, God only knows; I cannot
recall ever hearing them fall from his lips. Yet he was a man
of strong and constant loves. He was very fond of the landscapes of New England. The ways we trod in that summer-
time, quite new to me, were very familiar to him; and he
would interrupt a discussion, even a warm dispute, to make
sure that I was not missing some or other beautiful prospect.
It was the view as a whole, the composition of it, that he
liked to emphasize; for instance, a valley below us ascending slowly on our left through meadows to wooded heights,
but descending sharply on our right to where there was a
glimpse of a lake deep-set among hills, with the bald cone
of Monadnock towering close behind. After brief and
definite comments given in a low voice, he would contemplate the scene in silence for a moment, then turn abruptly
away from it; carrying it in his eyes, however, as he walked
along. But soon the resumed discussion would bring to the
fore an idea that he loved, and then the whole look of his
face would change, withdrawing and concentering, as
though, instead of the beautiful valley below, he was seeing
an unseen star in front: he would pause to watch it. There
were those two sorts of pause, the pause for the scene and

the pause for the idea. He absorbed the scene; the idea absorbed him. For him the scene, as not for Wordsworth in the famous walking sonnet, was just some happy tone (of Maya?) slipping in between the idea coming and the idea gone.

In exposing an idea he would often use a peculiar and significant gesture. His right hand, rising beside its shoulder with spread fingers and outward palm, would make short lateral pushes in the air. There was not the slightest volitant or undulatory motion of the arm—no concession to flying, no fluent gracefulness. Those shoves of the open hand off into space—into the spaces of thought—were rigid and impersonal. They insisted that the principle of which he was talking was patently universal, belonging to everyone and no one. As for wrong opposing notions, his fingers would sweep them down and away, one after another, while his tongue attacked them. In assailing a tendency which he considered "nothing less than pernicious" (one of his favorite phrases) his aspect would become nothing less than predaceous. The claw-like swoop of the hand, the metallic ring of the voice, the gnashing movement of the large irregular mouth, the thrusting jaw and commanding beak, would strike me into a dumb fascination as though I myself were the hapless prey. However, one noted also something indefinable in Babbitt's mien that stayed always above the combat, something that one associated with the upper part of his face, the large forehead and large blue eyes. I have never seen a pair of eyes that could so glint with the lust of battle while remaining at the same time so deeply imperturbable. They would fill with reverence when he was expatiating upon a great saint or sage. And sometimes the spread hand beside its shoulder would tilt slightly backwards as in a repressed or inchoate gesture of adoration.

But his moments of solemnity, even in intimate conversation, were very transient. Gravity was always there, but so was cheerfulness sparkling with quick and various wit. Certainly his style of talk (as in the case of Doctor Johnson) was far more flexible and alluring than his written style. His books have some passages of misplaced solemnity—owing, as one reviewer put it, with vast and solemn exaggeration, to "his attempt to apply philosophic first principles to every detail of modern life." [1] In his conversation, however, many a "detail of modern life" was treated with indulgent if satiric humor. One day I found him chuckling over the memory of a high Boston banquet at which he had been a guest on the previous evening. By way of appetizer and in spite of Prohibition, dashes of rare old rum were served in the bottoms of beautiful goblets. And many professorial faces at the table expressed a double question: what of the law of the land? and why so little drink in such a large container? The proper technique of course was, before sipping, to cherish the goblet in one's hands while inhaling the choice aroma with intruded nose. The awkwardness with which the guests performed, or omitted, this fine

[1] *The Times Literary Supplement* (London), December 8, 1932. Regarding the "higher will"—an old datum of human experience and treated as such by many careful thinkers before Babbitt—the reviewer asserts: "it seems necessary to wait upon psychology before one can decide whether there is such a thing." Well, a reviewer who can wait thus solemnly upon current psychology, towards which Babbitt's attitude was very far from solemn, would naturally be opaque to Babbitt's grave wit. And this case is typical. Many of Babbitt's reviewers, though writing with modernistic lightness, had solemnly swallowed some or other current doctrine which he attacked with witty penetration; and their response was, "He is hopelessly solemn"! Their solemniferous levity slubbered his witty gravity.

but then and there unaccustomed rite, was rendered by Babbitt with exquisite ludicrousness. I asked, "How did you yourself make out?"—"Oh, I sniffed the stuff properly enough."

His chief self-indulgence, perhaps, was laughter at self-indulgence. Gourmets tickled him immensely. And minor comfortablenesses that conventional people took for granted could set his big eyes twinkling. Once when we were discussing the subject of conditions favorable for literary composition, I let slip a piece of personal information that caused him to stare. "So you actually find it possible," he exclaimed, much amused, "to smoke while engaged in writing!" I was unable to see the joke. But presently I laughed when my fancy conjured up the impossible picture of Babbitt himself smoking while inditing, let's say, *Rousseau and Romanticism.*

After dinner he would smoke a cigar, but not with any succulency. The thing continually went out; and, perched as it was between two fingers of an open, jerkily gesturing hand, it seemed ever on the point of catapulting into space, if not into somebody's eye. However, the eyes of others were not in much danger from Babbitt. His demeanor was carefully polite, sometimes too carefully; for, sociable by nature, he had also a moral conviction of the value of polite society. One could watch that conviction sustaining him in parlors when his temper was being sorely tried. His sometime attitude at teas brings to my mind a line from Lear, "Pour on, I will endure." At teas or after dinner when the company's conversation waxed oppressively conventional, he would gaze thoughtfully at the carpet to hide the satire of his eyes. In extreme cases he was seized by a sudden elaborate interest in his neglected cigar; turning it about and pondering it; perchance scraping the burnt end with the edge of a match and then, unless the stub proved to be hopelessly short and soggy, relighting it with meticulous fingers. His voice all the while applied similar treatment to dull interlocutors. They were not butts for his ridicule, they were beings to be relighted, if at all possible, with all possible patience.

That sort of person would often play up to him, praising his doctrines to his face, but then drawing narrow conclusions or adducing empty instances, prefaced maybe with a "Yes, Professor Babbitt, and don't you also think that" —etc.

"Uh—not precisely," he would respond and then proceed to formulate a scrupulous distinction. He had much to endure from such querists. Sometimes they forced him to laugh, but the laugh, even when behind their backs, was restrained and considerate. He wished not to damage any thread of conventional thought that had any validity to it. Such threads were the social warp, and he wished them, instead of being broken after the modernistic fashion, to be rewoven into a firmly modern pattern; particularly in America, where there was special opportunity for just such a pattern and special danger without it. "Pestiferous" was his word for American visionaries who naïvely echoed the subversive doctrines that had grown so noisy in older countries by way of reaction from old intrenched habits. Those doctrines when transferred into new and mobile America were, he often exclaimed, "thoroughly pestilential." He ridiculed the "imported notion" that the *chief* danger of modern America was moribund conventionalism. Radicals who cherished that notion stirred him to raucous mirth; which would subside into a gentle chuckling when his mind turned to the opposite sect, hidebound respectable persons. These pestered him considerably; but they were not "pestiferous."

"Of course," I heard him say more than once, before I noticed the same epigram in his writings, "where there is no vision the people perish, but where there is sham vision they perish even faster." Accordingly he attacked wrong visions rather than wrong actions. For him all conduct in the long run was the result of vision, of imaginatized ideas. The Great War was the foreseen result of certain bad ideas that he had been tracing down through the nineteenth century; and the course of the War interested him less than the course of those ideas. He was never tired of declaiming upon the unethical twist in the imagination of the time of Wordsworth, so fruitful, he thought, of ill results at the present day. But he pooh-poohed the fuss that arose upon the discovery of that poet's liaison with Annette Vallon. Why refuse to recognize a malady in the plant and then get loudly excited over the withering of a petal? He was far more intolerant of warped ideas than of irregular conduct.

He was tolerant of Bohemian ways in persons who were at once sincere and large. Unable to conceive of himself as large, he wished to be socially regular, even personally unobtrusive; and perhaps he succeeded as well as nature would permit. In this connection I recall his first visit in my home when I subjected him, in right American fashion, to an overdose of entertainment. Between two sieges of company he informed me very brusquely that he was going for a solitary walk. As the time was short, the vicinity new to him, and his love of walking notorious, I warned him against straying too far. Rejecting the warning as entirely uncalled for, he turned his back and marched away. When, close upon dinnertime, he failed to reappear, I made search with an automobile in the gathering twilight and came upon him, not very far off, returning at hot-foot speed. With difficulty I persuaded him to get into the car. He was much annoyed at being mechanically retrieved, engined into a status of social delinquency. He laid claim to punctuality, arguing the point with Johnsonian sophistry.

In his later years his side face reminded me often of the miniature of Doctor Johnson made familiar to Americans by Professor C. B. Tinker. But while highly admiring Johnson's character, Babbitt had no fond indulgence for his rude obtrusiveness, any more than he had for the subtler arrogance of his Victorian successor, the admirable Arnold. As for the moody egotism of minor British celebrities visiting in America, accentuated as it was by modern Bohemianism, he could ridicule it deliciously. He wished America to retain the moral robustness of the Anglo-Saxons while leaving behind their insular arrogancy. In social attitude we Americans could well take lessons, he would urge, from the French and the Chinese. He dubbed the Chinese "the English of the Orient" on account of their innate good sense, but he loved to enlarge upon the superiority of their religious tradition of good manners. He deplored the current decline in China of Confucian scholarship; he conferred much upon this matter with the Chinese students who came to work under him. The rehabilitation of China seemed to him an extremely important task for the sake, not just of that country, but of society at large.

His talk passed rapidly from land to land, from age to age, and from sage to sage. His listeners came to realize, far more vividly than those who knew him only in his writings, that here was a man who habitually thought of the world as a unit and of human history as a single worldwide process. American cosmopolitanism—a phrase which he disliked because of its cheap connotations—attained in him a high and firm level. It freed him from that deep-set

European mentality which accentuates, even while trying to override, the line between East and West. It stationed his mind, as naturally as the American continent, between Europe and what Europe has termed "the Far East." It enabled him to talk of Confucius and Buddha with the same unforced intimacy as of Aristotle and St. Paul. It freed him of course from nationalism, but not from nationality. Sentimental internationalism, especially the American brand, seemed to him an even greater danger than occidental jingoism. And he loved America with a love as deep and working as it was unproclaimed. Often after a loud-jibing pessimistic analysis of some or other American evil, he would lean his head towards me and say in a low tone, "But of course my hope for America is better than my words." And here let it be recorded that though he admired the French language, knew it thoroughly, and spoke it fluently, he spoke it ever with an accent that was nakedly Yankee and utterly unashamed.

He was American in his restless energy. His life was a restless campaign against American restlessness—a battling effort to turn our thinking towards the Supreme Peace. That paradox was vital; disease germs have to be fought with conditioned germs of the same disease. Hence his unfailing devotion to Harvard University, even the modern Harvard, our leading American factory for mental mass production. He himself was a distinguished product of that mill; distinguished, because from the outset the Buddha, instead of President Eliot, had played the dominant part in the shaping process. Babbit once pointed out to me, with a mien of gratitude to fate, an avenue in the outskirts of Cambridge where as a young undergraduate he had been wont to trot back and forth holding a Pali text to his eyes, learning its language and absorbing its lore while exercising his legs. "A running

study of Buddha," I silently reflected; the still image of
that sage arose in my mind, and I marveled at the reincarnation of the ancient Hindu spirit in a current Harvard
American. Reincarnation is not too strong a word, for
Babbitt's beliefs came from within himself far more than
from his studies. But this fact was unrecognized by him
because (in addition to his humility) he was from first to
last a Harvard scholar busily investigating innumerable
texts. He documented his deepest insights as conscien-
tiously as others cited authorities for the shallowest facts.
He wanted the Higher Will to be as carefully researched
as, let's say, the last will of Shakespeare. In his talk Har-
vardian scholasticism was satirized and defended with a
quickness of alternation that disconcerted his listeners.
Woe to them if their criticism of his university smacked of
dilettantism, for this sin was worse in his eyes than the dry-
as-dustiest pedantry. He shared, and strove to elevate, the
Germanic energeia of his Alma Mater. Harvard in his view
was the main station for receiving and converting the elec-
trical currents of American thought.

"What we need today in American crit'c'sm," I can still
hear him saying in his clipped pronunciation, "is the historical tracing of great formative tendencies." America,
now inundated with contemporaneity, must rediscover the
noblest heights of thought in the past, the whole long past,
occidental and oriental, of which she is the inheritor. Nor
can those heights appear to us commandingly (so he would
argue) unless our critical thinking sets itself sharply against
the errors of modern naturalism, to which American civilization, so largely a creature of the modern age, is peculiarly
exposed. In other words the modern American critic, if he
is to build firmly, must also firmly destroy. This point he
pressed upon me in the earlier days of our acquaintance

when he still had hope that I too would be warlike. Once, after a long dispute, he fell silent for a while, then thrust his head towards me and said in a grimly humorous tone, "At least it seems that you and I agree that what America needs today is a new deal in ideas?"

"Very true."

"Well, then," he exclaimed loudly, shaking his fist at things in general—and in that moment I felt like a thing in general—"why don't you get out and fight?" These words were uttered with an inward, mounting forcefulness that cannot be put on paper. After many years, I hear an eternal echo, "get-out-and-FIGHT."

His talk forced younger academics to face their danger of yielding to the American lust for being in the swim. They might easily and insensibly lower their standards while disguising this weakness under a benevolent desire to encourage contemporary art and letters in America. But surely, his listener would urge, such encouragement is needed: we must have a native literature. He would reply satirically that our journalists could be trusted to flatter all that was second-rate in American "creative" writing. The function of the teacher and academic critic was to prepare the way for a first-rate American art to come. This could be done only by placing the emphasis on sound ideas and high standards—not on art for art's sake, not on what Babbitt called "the merely lit'r'y aspects."

His personal lack of interest in current imaginative writings was well-nigh complete. His chief recreation in solitude was the reading of classic passages of poetry and prose in various languages, above all the Greek. One day when he was on the point of setting out for a badly needed vacation in Europe, he confided to me that the finest pleasure that he proposed for himself over there, was a rereading of Sophocles while strolling upon the Acropolis. He made this confession shyly, glancing sideways at me to see if its touch of romantic-classical sentiment would bring a smile to my lips. But I could not smile; I was seeing two moving pictures—one of a cantering youth engrossed in the aphorisms of Buddha in the outskirts of flat Cambridge; the other, of an elderly and overworked scholar pondering high Greek drama among the ruins on the sacred Athenian hill. . . . Leisure for him was a change of mental work. He would laugh derisively when informed that such and such a professor of literature was accustomed at times to regale himself with detective stories. He interrogated me upon my lighter reading and chuckled immensely over some of the items I confessed. "But," I declared, "one cannot be always occupied with the grand old masters and the bards sublime. You, when you are utterly fagged after a day's work—what do you read then?"

"Contemp'r'y crit'c'sm," he replied simply. And indeed he had an amazing acquaintance with that field. He perused it at once for amusement and for refutation. Often he would snatch up from his table some brand new critical book or article, read aloud to me its most wrong-headed passage, and then define the particular brand of romanticism or naturalism represented by the author. I averred maliciously that it was a waste of time to read such ephemeral stuff, that it ought to be allowed to die a natural death; why throw harpoons at skyrockets? By way of reply he threw several at me. Those "skyrockets," he asserted, could dazzle and mislead a great many readers, particularly in America where the reading public was extraordinarily naïve. Surely, then, an American critic, if he was in earnest, should attack current critical errors instead of waiting for them to die or, rather—unlike "skyrockets," this being a false metaphor—to take root in the soil.

"A critic," he said, "must understand his function. He dare not aim at future readers. Of course any writer who is worth his salt hopes to be read after his death. But it is the critic's business to grapple with the age in which he lives and give it what he sees it needs."

"Very well," I said, "but some of us wish that you would write one book, just one, in which, laying aside your critico-historical methods—omitting all reference to the works of others—you would give your message in a direct, personal manner."

He stared at me and laughed. "You'd like me to essay the role of prophet or confessor?"

"Not exactly, but—"

"We have too many prophets and confessors already; that is just the trouble with the modern age. No, no," he concluded with sharp finality of tone, "my critical function is a humble one but, I believe, necessary."

Sometimes, as I have just suggested, Babbitt would override or sidestep an objection; and then one would reflect how extraordinary it was that he did not do so oftener, considering his pugnacity. His principle—not consistently followed, else he had been unhuman—was *not* to "talk for victory," that is for personal triumph. He would not use his power of wit crushingly if he perceived that his questioner was impersonally seeking truth, however much at his expense. He would submit patiently to grueling cross-examinations upon dubious passages in his writings; and in the end he would often say mildly, "I shall try to make that matter clearer in my next book." More often, however, he would respond with questions that led his questioner into a

Socratic trap. As for trapping him, that was an Herculean labor. Only once in the whole course of our conversations do I recall his being nonplussed. He had been inveighing against the many who employ the slogan of "service to mankind" to advance their own selfish interests. I remarked, with studied seriousness, "As a rule you insist on a very discriminating use of categorical terms, such as 'humanist'—"

"Yes, yes?"

"But just now you have employed the term 'humanitarian' very indiscriminately." I repeated some of his assertions.

"Ye-e-es," he replied slowly, "yes, that is so." Then he went on with a rush, "But they happen to be my chief aversion, I simply cannot stand them—the humanitarian boosters." His right hand performed an orbit of comprehensive denunciation; his tone was almost a bark. "Cerberus," I murmured at him, and he was mildly amused. He was richly amused by the vivid invections of H. L. Mencken against the American booster. He would quote them with delight; then proceed to criticize that writer's *Weltanschauung;* and then, mayhap, cite one of Mencken's clever thrusts at Professor Babbitt.

He could laugh at himself with entire lack of constraint, with a serene gleam in his eyes that played upon himself as one of the transient Many. I recall his mirth when there came to his ears the following local witticism upon his local status: "Babbitt's fame is going round the world, it has already left Cambridge." I remember when he repeated, chuckling, a journalist's word picture of him searching spinsterishly under his bed each night for Rousseau. One day I came across him after his return from a large Phi Beta Kappa gathering in another city, where he and a certain prominent university president had been the only speakers.

The president, of course, spoke first, taking for his subject "The Value of Ideals." This, Babbitt told me, was a trifle embarrassing since his own address was to be on "The Value of Standards as Opposed to Ideals." But he had proceeded to deliver it without any modifications. The humor with which he recounted the episode was entirely impartial; it placed the two discordant orators in the same box. I wondered just how the prominent university president felt while listening to the second speaker; but Babbitt refused to wonder.

He had small interest in the art of conciliation; he did not like it practiced on him and would not practice it on others. Caring as little for its twin, the art of correspondence—letters are a kind of "conciliation" (literally, a drawing together)—he made his letters as few and brief as possible, claiming that this was for him a necessary way of saving time. An old friend to whom he had occasion to forward annually a sum of money complained, "I get no word from you except the Inner Check." Not so humorous and indulgent were other would-be correspondents. As his fame increased they poured in upon him an increasing stream of mail and did not relish receiving few or no words in reply. Babbitt wished his admirers to correspond with his ideas rather than with him. Once he showed me an engaging missive which I urged him to answer at once. It was from a budding critic who seemed to me exceptionally gifted and who certainly evinced an ardent interest in Babbitt and his ideas. Later on, I was astonished to come across in print a warm attack upon those very ideas by the selfsame writer. I asked Babbitt just what he had written in answer to the young man's letter. "Nothing," he replied coolly, "I did not find the time." He laughed at my blank look. But I, quoting Emerson's epigram, "In youth we are mad for persons," urged that young people normally come to truth through an interest in persons who have it, an interest that should not be discouraged. He rejoined, it was equally obvious that a young man was not on the way to becoming a worth-while critic if his interest in sound ideas could be easily discouraged and if he persisted in maintaining a youthful disposition to be mad for persons, or at them.

Persons and ideas were sharply distinguished in Babbitt's mind. Often one heard him denounce a man's ideas while expressing a sincere regard for the man himself. This attitude was inadequately reciprocated by his colleagues in academe. When their personal interests were grazed by his heavy impersonal tread they were apt to discount him by declaring that he lacked the true professorial balance: preacher rather than scholar, he properly belonged outside the academic pale. At the same time, comically enough, he was being hotly consigned to the *inside* of that pale by his journalistic opponents: for them he was a dangerous incarnation of the essence of professorialism. And surely their instinct was the right one. Babbitt was turning a high-pressure hose (such was the picture that came to my mind) upon incendiary notions that threatened the very citadel of academe—while other academics, upon whose toes he had trodden en route to the fire, complained that his way of holding the nozzle was quite unacademic. "Babbitt," I heard Professor X assert, "is a mere propagandist." The hiss with which the "ist" was uttered seemed to me unnatural, till I learned later that Babbitt was known to have remarked that X's ideas were "critically negligible." More than once, however, I heard Babbitt praise X highly for character and ability. Indeed, undervaluing his own talents, he was apt to overestimate those of other persons; espe-

cially in the case of his friends. He had a genius for friendship. Greatly occupied as he was, he would go out of his
way to serve the interest of friends who did not do the like
for him.

Unfortunately, at least from the contemporary standpoint, his personal generosity was not so apparent in his
writings since there he was preoccupied with ideas and
tendencies. In conversation he could praise discerningly
the charms and incidental insights not only of J. J. Rousseau but of present-day "naturists." When he took pen in
hand, however, all other considerations were overshadowed
by his conviction that the central tendency of these writers
was fatefully wrong. I was disturbed by his very sharp
review of a certain popular and rather distinguished book
on morals. His handling of it, I told him, was plainly lop-
sided and had doubtless resulted in the addition of a new
battalion to his large army of enemies. He replied that the
book was fundamentally wrong, built upon a confusion of
humanism and stoicism, and that this fact, ignored by other
reviewers, had to be emphasized by him. I retorted that he
himself had ignored several good points in the book, for
instance, the exceptionally sensible treatment of sex.

"A sound treatment of sex," Babbitt rejoined severely,
"requires a religious background which this author does
not possess. At this point, at least, I seem to put more emphasis on religion than you do." (I had recently been ac-
cusing him of not giving religion its due.) Presently he
called my attention to a new work which, unlike the one
just mentioned, he heartily approved of. In reading it I
soon discovered that the writer had liberally helped himself
to Babbitt's philosophy without once mentioning his name.
I said to him ironically, "This work would naturally interest you, its ideas are your own—in disguise."

"I did not look at the matter that way," he replied with entire simplicity. "My impression is that this writer is one who thinks things out for himself." He added that, on account of his unpopularity with the reviewers, new authors who were in favor of humanistic ideas could get a better hearing if they refrained from bringing in his name. That, he said, employing one of his favorite military metaphors—that was "good tactics." On the same grounds, those who showed intentions of dedicating books to him, he urged not to do so. Even a group of his former students who planned, in accordance with a pleasant academic custom, to produce a symposium in his honor, relinquished their purpose, so unmistakably sincere was his disapproval of it.

No doubt his rare disinterestedness was favored by his rare defect of the artistic temperament; he was not a thin-skinned person. But he was far from impassible; and the accumulated hostility aroused by his lifework was not an easy burden for him in his last years. "Fighting a whole generation," he remarked to me in an intimate moment, "is not exactly a happy task." He added somberly, "I have had to live at a time when all the ideas which I know to be most vital for man have more and more declined." He could not see, because of his essential modesty, that his own case was a powerful instance to the contrary. I spoke of his influence, asserting that it had seeped further and deeper than appeared. But he discounted it heavily, repeating my word "seep" with a scornful grunt. Not seeping but rousing to battle was the effect he aimed at. The time was one of great human crisis: the enemy truly were plenteous, but humanistic fighters were few. In short, he wanted more Irving Babbitts—not realizing how difficult he was for Providence to duplicate—and he was distressed by their persistent refusal to appear. He had an increasing sense of loneliness in his warfare. When our walk one day took us near a cemetery he waved a finger at it and muttered with dark satisfaction, "That puts a man in mind of his rest."

Such somber notes, however, were utterly exceptional. His talk and, I am sure, his thoughts were seldom concerned with his own career. Yet the more closely one came to know him, the more one could see that he had a large capacity for personal ambition and for all the feelings, good and ill, that attend it. But one perceived at the same time that he was vigilantly at work subduing his personal desires to the "Higher Will." His incessant "inner working" was never on display; it was veiled from others by the steady cheerfulness to which it gave rise; and it was veiled from himself, so to speak, by the steady humility which gave rise to it. Never in our most intimate talks did he allude confessionally to his own spiritual efforts: I saw that he regarded them as, essentially, not his own. He looked in with humility—even while looking out with pride. He had the natural self-pride of a man of strong feelings strongly under control, a pride sometimes touched with harsh scorn of human follies and weaknesses. But the scorn was momentary, and the pride was overshadowed by his high reverence for the unseen Law. That supernatural Law and Will (for it was both of these at once) became for him in his later years ever more of a real presence. During one of our last walks, his mind dwelt exceptionally upon the old theme of human transience; till finally he exclaimed, with bent head and raised hand, with a depth of simple awe, entirely devoid of any note of fatalism or personal mournfulness, "Oh, God is very great and a man is a worm."

After a silence, I said, "But the God whom men worship is not just a Will, as in your writings, but a Being, a complete Being, who—"

"Yes, yes," he broke in with humorous impatience, "but that is beyond my province as a writer. Why do you keep wishing me to be a theologian? I am merely a critic." And surely (he proceeded) the critical point in regard to religion, especially today, was that divine reality, whatever else it might be, could not be real to men unless they found it at work in themselves as a Will commanding their own wills. . . . He spoke impersonally, with profound personal conviction. "Merely a critic," he called himself; he never knew how much more than a critic he was; and that unawareness was part of his great dedication. He would be much abashed, he would rebuke me severely, if he knew that, as I reflect upon him, I recall the parable of the man to whom the Master of the Feast said, "Friend, go up higher."

Certain of Babbitt's writings will be dealt with in the course of the fifth chapter, below. They may be seen in better perspective after considering the work of his friend, the late Paul E. More, and his brilliant pupil, the late Stuart Sherman.

3.

Paul E. More and the Gentle Reader

N OT LONG AGO A PERIODICAL ARTICLE GAVE VENT TO A
confident but rather cryptic opinion upon Paul
Elmer More. In effect, it was this: Mr. More is a very distinguished critic, but he is not pertinent to our age. No
irony was intended against "our age," which, indeed, the
writer of the article identified with his own. He did not
stop to reflect that pertinency is ambidextrous and that
"our age," in finding "a very distinguished critic" not pertinent to it, might prove itself impertinent to him. Nevertheless, my conviction is that in recent years we have been
insensibly drawing closer to More's position, that his work
has for us a heightening pertinency which needs just now
to be clearly seen and admitted. But, first, let us face this
question: Why is it that so far he has been treated by "our
age" with even more reluctance or hostility than has usually fallen to the lot of a "very distinguished critic"?

Certainly he is among the leading critics in the English
language; let us say, for the sake of safety and conciliation,
among the leading dozen. Just as certainly, none of the
other eleven in their day and generation has made less appeal to the "gentle reader." This term is out of date but the
personage himself is still with us. He may be, for example,
a balancing academic who feels that More is much too decided, perhaps too narrow and unsympathetic, certainly

too much addicted to critical categories and labels; who, for his own part, heartily dislikes labels but innocently wears, still, the label of the "Culture" of Matthew Arnold, still trying to see life vaguely and see it whole. Or, he may be a vital onrusher, devoted to what he calls "life"; heartily disliking academics, but too "gentle" in his power of mental discrimination to perceive the gulf that divides More from them. Or he may be . . . But, enough! The plain fact is that More is an extraordinarily severe thinker who has come at a time when severity of thought, in the field of literature, is extraordinarily out of fashion.

Intellectual softness pervades our literary atmosphere like carbon monoxide. We breathe it unaware. The situation is quite climactic. During the past two centuries intellectual severity has gone over more and more from literature into science. This process has culminated in our age. Literature today is nebulae in the outskirts of the solid-seeming universe of science. Our literature is soft, soft.

We do not like to admit this fact in all its blankness, for the instinct of the human army is to conceal its losses. We have wished to believe that there is something primitively vigorous in the jets of feeling and runlets of fancy that flow so quaintly in our characteristic writings. Thus, our luckless poets and novelists have been encouraged to cultivate an overstrained style, unique in the history of literature and destined for the laughter of future generations. In particular, a smoky imagery of sex, soft, acrid, and voluminous, has been poured forth to conceal the trivial fire of passion in the green veins of our authors. Perhaps never before have such authors been treated by reviewers and readers so gently. Our aversion to the term "gentle reader" is, in psychological parlance, a defense mechanism. We suppress the term because the thing itself has got into our

very marrow and we are subconsciously ashamed of it. We
are, but do not wish to appear, extremely gentle readers.

Well, More insists we are. In one way or another, for a
quarter of a century, he has relentlessly uncovered our se-
cret awareness of our literary and spiritual softness. He has
not been tactful about it. Perhaps no important critic in the
past has been equally lacking in the art of conciliating current readers. He is devoid of even the most innocent flat-
teries. One reason for this is his extreme personal modesty
as a writer. For example, classic ideas that other modern
critics have suavely given forth as their own are carefully
assigned by More to classic authors. He has made echo elo-
quent, and the reviewers hoarse, with repetition of his
Plato's name even while quietly shaping forth a deeply
original Platonism answering to a central modern need.
Other critics, in rediscovering and reshaping an ancient
idea, have known how to intimate their own originality.
Doctor Johnson, Coleridge, and Arnold, with the underlying aid, no doubt, of British arrogance, were fully competent in the polite art of cackling. But More's style refuses the faintest cluck. In rereading the *Shelburne Essays*
one finds many a passage of fresh and profound thinking
that had previously been concealed (and is now revealed)
by the austerest simplicity and impersonality of style. This
critic waives entirely that gentle mixture of advertisement
and flattery which the modern reader condones and demands. Time, as I have hinted, may justify More's method
fully—but not our time. To refuse to conciliate our spirits
even while showing how soft our spirits have become, to
demonstrate the rawness of our nerves by firmly walking
over them—well, our relief has been to loathe him or, at
the least, to claim that he is not pertinent to our age.

Yet it now appears that the age is swinging in More's

general direction. I should like to state this curious phenomenon in its lowest and plainest terms. But I hesitate to utter the abrupt sentence that arises in me. It may cause all gentle readers to start from their armchairs and scream "Treason! Treason!" and to "look pale and tremble at this chance" as the company in the final scene of *Hamlet* are supposed to do when King Claudius is stabbed. In their heart of hearts, however, the courtly company is, no doubt, much relieved. Claudius, with his monotonous repetition of poisonous wiles, is a tiresome fellow, at least on the modern stage. No one is very sorry when he receives a friendly thrust somewhere near his chest and is carried off stage to doff his royal robes. Somewhat similar is the case of Nature, as modernly interpreted; and, when the initial shock is over, we gentle readers, in our heart of hearts, shall be glad of this treasonable confession: We are getting thoroughly bored with King Nature.

The attempt to explain all of human life in terms of natural science has now achieved a monotony so sovereign as utterly to overshadow the medieval attempt to explain it all in terms of Latin theology. The reason should be obvious. God and Nature are both essential for human versatility, if for nothing higher. They provide the fundamental variety of Man. If either of these two grand factors is omitted or submerged, our life begins to flatten out. Our literature becomes a stagnant pool, relieved only by vapors, rank or ethereal vapors as the case may be. Such is the divine human irony. But it goes deeper. The human mind is so constituted that it can easily waive God but not Nature. Nature we have always with us; Him, not always. Therefore, when we concentrate our attention entirely upon Nature we take the way of least resistance toward complete ennui. The twentieth century has already succeeded in making itself, spiritually, what the thirteenth century, with all its dreadful faults, never was and never could have had the ghost of a chance of becoming—namely, a triumphant bore.

Just here some gentle reader may shake a finger at me and squeak, "Ah, ha, medievalist!" However, I dislike medievalism. What we need is not a retreat to the Middle Ages but a strenuous recovery from our own unexampled retreat into Nature. In this connection, we have to face the grand paradox suggested above. In the twentieth century, a vast official preoccupation with man's natural desires has been accompanied by a decline of healthy vigor in those very desires. In the thirteenth century, a vast official preoccupation with divinity was accompanied by a huge vigor in man's natural desires. They surged and beat about the Great White Throne. The cool Sea of Glass constructed by scholastic philosophy was strictly limited in acreage. Ambition and sex-love could be assigned to Dante's hell, but not denied or emasculated by any Christian, or behavioristic, "science." Hell, in fact, was boldly regarded as part of the divine will. In other words, there was full recognition of the hell and the heaven in human nature, mysteriously co-operant and opposed.

It was thus that the thirteenth century prepared the great dramatic energies of the Renaissance. Shakespeare's work is the medieval outlook in full-blown secular form. He was a child of Nature and had no use for otherworldliness. But in the very blood of his brain was the conviction that two different worlds, or natures, meet in man. Hence the scope and variety of his vision, the intense reality of his contrasts. All his contrasts are fed from one central contrast. He knew by heart the central contrariety of human nature, the opposition between passion and that higher reach of our spirit that is above passion's sway. His great successor, Milton, took up this theme and developed it to its poetic utmost. He envisaged the human duality, so to call it, in sublime images of dark and bright. . . . And More has carried it through the length and breadth of his critical writings; as when (to choose an example almost at random) he remarks upon "the consciousness, which no reasoning of philosophy and no noise of the world can ever quite obliterate, of two opposite principles in us, one bespeaking unity and peace and infinite life, the other calling us to endless change and division and discord."

It is not improper to bring More into so quick a juxtaposition with Milton. A thing that Milton did for English poetry, More has done for English criticism. He has established therein, with rare philosophic rigor and penetration, the idea of the human duality. Other literary critics have surpassed him in other ways; no other has equaled him in this way. Johnson, Coleridge, and Arnold are beyond him in intensity of esthetic response and in richness of personality. Johnson had a wittier force, Coleridge a more brilliant imagination, Arnold a fuller urbanity. But when compared with More they appear somewhat childlike in the art of philosophy. We must go to Milton's prose works to match the analytic power, the width of investigation, and the solidity of statement that appear in More's *Greek Tradition*. Like Milton, More had to face the task of rescuing philosophy for literature. Milton tried to rescue it from the sects of theologic metaphysicians. More has rescued it from a confusion worse confounded, namely, the metaphysics of science environed with spiritual fog.

In doing so, he has exhibited, however differently, that combination of Greek thought and Puritan will which characterized Milton but was not maintained by his successors in English literature. In the eighteenth century, English Hellenism was conventional. In the nineteenth, it was fresh, inflated, confused, and, finally, rotten. It had plenty of "good will" but not strong and strict will. It was shaken to the very center by the new flood of naturistic thought and feeling which it attempted to embrace and direct. Even Emerson in his rockbound New England, remote from the European imbroglio, was half swamped, mentally, by the billows of modern Nature. Certainly he had the Puritan will in his life, but not in the main development of his thought. His ideas swirled loose from it. A brother Puritan, Carlyle, came storming down from Scotland to London and tried to clear the metropolitan air with thunder. But the barometer was too low; and his own mind was too foggy. If Concord was too far from London—so a cynic might remark—Scotland was too near. Whatever capacity Carlyle had earlier shown for philosophic progress was now beclouded. He shouted graphically on behalf of Jehovah and the old-time Devil. But he could not re-form them for the modern intellect.

To realize what a strait English imaginative thought had come into, we have only to reflect upon this: the chief moral force current in English literature was endowed, in the seventeenth century, with the mind of Milton; in the nineteenth century, with the mind of Carlyle! This prophet, and he was a real prophet, had no way to meet the new naturistic Hellenism except by despising it. If Carlyle had been an intellectual match for Emerson, the subsequent course of literary thought might have been less misty. But the palm, so far as intellection was concerned, went to Yankee Hellenism. In other words, the most potent imaginative thought of the past hundred years was created by one who, in his quite provincial reaction from Puritanism, obscured the significance of the Puritan will. The effect appeared, diversely, in Emerson's disciples Matthew Arnold and Walt Whitman. They adapted his blunder to academic and journalistic palates, respectively, and did much to establish it for the twentieth century.

What our age needed, therefore, was a severe critical revision of Yankee Hellenism or, more politely, of New England Humanism. This has been provided by Paul E. More and his compeer, Irving Babbitt. They had the Puritan will in themselves and they succeeded in translating it into literary thought. Divesting it of Latinistic theology [1] and of Protestant moralism, they have brought it into vital relation with the best of Greek and Hindu philosophy. The Sixth Series of the *Shelburne Essays, Studies of Religious Dualism*, which appeared in 1909, was a quietly momentous book for our time. It represented the Christian conception of the dual will of man, the Sin and Grace so heavily accented by the Puritans, as merely one form of a perennial human experience that is central, not only in religion, but in literature; that constitutes, in fact, the most vital source of the human imagination.

Certainly this truth was not unknown to More's predecessors in English criticism after Milton. But they did not know it so poetically as Milton, nor with such power of discrimination as More. They did not establish it in valid modern terms. Johnson knew it firmly, but he knew it narrowly. Coleridge knew it loftily, but he knew it cloudily. Arnold knew it politely but, alas, he knew it softly! The gentility or, shall we say, the "genteelity," of his touch upon the duality of the human spirit was symptomatic and ominous. The progressive softening of that great truth during the modern era has meant the progressive softening

[1] This was written before More's final theological phase.

of literature until now. There is a certain excitement in the fact that this American critic, in an age of natural science, has carried the sting and cogency of science into literary thought and has thereby rejuvenated an old human truth.

The interest grows when we note that just now the so solid-seeming universe, created by physical science during the past two centuries, is beginning to melt and shimmer. When a sober scientist declares that space must be considered round but unlimited, he is in agreement with the imaginative science of John Milton. Indeed, it seems that science may presently succeed in demonstrating what the great poets and sages always knew: that material nature is an "insubstantial pageant," a vision of the mind. But, in this case, what becomes of the bulk of contemporary literature? Its interest has hung upon a vivid contrast between the solidity of physical nature and the fluidity of human nature. The "stream of consciousness," to which our writers have more and more devoted themselves, has had a gross, material Nature to flow around. Now, however, this Nature is itself in flux. The "stream of consciousness" becomes thus a pageant shimmering around a pageant; nebulae whirling about nebulae; streams encircling streams, like the rivers in Milton's hell, "a watery labyrinth."

No wonder we gentle readers are bored with Nature, inner and outer—with the modern King Nature and his labyrinthine ways. Gentle as we are, we rebel when too heavily flooded with watery monotony. We demand in literature, for animation and variety if for nothing higher, some reality of contrast. We do not find this in a sheer, flowing tangle of variegated appetites. We know, from our own most inward experiences, that the essential contrast is between appetite and a region above appetite. We perceive that our writers need to regain a sense of "that element in

man which is outside of 'nature' and is denoted by consciously directive purpose." So says More in his volume
The Demon of the Absolute. Not that the literary artist
should turn moral or religious preacher. No, he must be
intimately concerned with "a world shaken by passionate
ambition and furious desire." But the very condition of
strong passion in literature is that the writer should find in
himself a standpoint above passion. The true artist is "one
who, by the subtle insinuating power of the imagination
. . . gives us always to feel that the true universal in human
nature is that part of man that is 'noble in reason,' the master and not the slave of passion. True art is thus humanistic
rather than naturalistic; and its gift of high and permanent
pleasure is the response of our own breast to the artist's
delicately revealed sense of that divine control, moving like
the spirit of God upon the face of the waters."

§ 2

"High and permanent pleasure". . . . That phrase returned to my mind when, after More's death, I began sadly
to reread his letters to me. The sadness retired before the
living vigor and clear beauty of his penned words. Some
day, I hope, his complete correspondence will be collected
and published. He was a voluminous and distinguished letter writer, unlike his friend Irving Babbitt, who was a distinguished and voluminous talker. Babbitt left with me a
pile, a volcanic pile, of conversational memories but only a
few dozen words set down with pen and ink. More wrote
me a considerable pile of letters, but my personal recollec-
tions of him are scant and rather pale. To be sure, my meetings with him were few and far between. But in his letters
I find his ideas far more pungently expressed than in his

conversation. He was first and last a writer. The "Hermit of Princeton," as he was dubbed, confided to friends that the moment of most intense delight in his daily life was the early-morning moment when he lifted his pen from his desk. He was not afflicted with writers' cramp—the mental kind, I mean. When he took pen in hand he did not gnaw the hither end of it, wondering what he was going to write. He knew just what he wanted to say and, in a rare degree, just how he was going to say it. In his letters as in his essays he conveys the feeling that was his when he was inditing them, a feeling of "high and permanent pleasure."

Not that he was unsociable; quite the contrary. Like Babbitt he was a very companionable person; but with a marked difference. The "Warring Buddha of Harvard," if one may so call Babbitt, regarded writing as mainly a duty. Comparatively speaking it was a hard and wearing task for him. If one called his attention to an obscure or jerky passage in a new essay of his, he would say: "Well, now, I tried very hard to make that clear; I thought it would read right along." My impression was that when he came out from his study after a bout of composition, he emerged into a larger freedom, the freedom of bouts of argument, bringing out high thoughts with which to assail his company. Not so the "Hermit of Princeton." In his study, alone with his pen, he had said his highest and completest say. In company he was very much the pleasant man of the world; carefully attired, physically and mentally; lending an ear to gossip, recounting in his turn amusing anecdotes; witty, urbane, and even suave. He seemed at times anxious to display to his listeners a genial indulgence that he denied to his readers. He covered his severe philosophy with a conversational lid. This, now and then, would lift a little to let out an acid phrase, accompanied by a half sardonic smile; but quickly the lid went down again and the smile smoothed-up its corners. Just because he was so much a hermit of the study he wished not to be alone when he was in company.

However, it is well known that with a single friend or in a select group More could doff his urbane manner and let out his inmost thoughts. Persons who, unlike me, were with him frequently should have much to record of him in this vein. Such records together with his letters are of special value in view of More's extraordinary personal reticence in his essays. . . . I have one recollection that I wish to set down here. When en route to a lecture engagement he spent several hours alone with me in my study. At that time he had entered upon his theological phase; I had written him a critical letter; he was warm with his new convictions; and the weather was provokingly hot. He accepted a glass of cold milk, nothing else; and somewhat to my surprise he took off his coat and rolled up his white shirt-sleeves. "Now," he said grim-smilingly, with a light flourish of his right arm, as though wielding a rapier—(instead of Babbitt's broadsword)—"now you will please to tell me plainly your religious beliefs and I shall then inform you just what sort of heretic you are!"

I told, or tried to tell, and he proceeded to pierce me through and through, sipping his milk the while. I could not well parry his swift logic nor hold my ground against his amazing knowledge of the history of theology, orthodox and unorthodox. He so fascinated me that I forgot the heat. But now I have also forgotten "just what sort of heretic" I was. In fact, it seems that I was several sorts all mixed up together. At first he set me down as an out-and-out Arian, but I protested firmly and he partly allowed my protest. On one point, at least, we were entirely agreed:

namely, that Arianism, if it is thought through to its proper conclusion, means that there can be nothing eternal, nothing without beginning or end, in the human spirit.

More's final position in respect to Christian theology is most tellingly given, I think, in the small book *The Skeptical Approach to Religion* [2] designed to summarize and simplify the argument developed in the six volumes of *The Greek Tradition*. But the uninitiated reader would perhaps do well to begin with the last chapter, the beautiful and moving essay on "The Gift of Hope," where the author, as a rule so shy of speaking autobiographically, comes very near to doing so. I confess that I approach this whole matter very gingerly, recalling Spenser's verse regarding the New Jerusalem, "Too high a ditty for my simple song." A full and careful study of More's theology has been provided by Professor Robert Shafer in his book, *Paul Elmer More and American Criticism*.[3] I have to offer a few remarks from a somewhat different point of view. I cannot share Professor Shafer's regret that More finally leaves his readers, after a fashion, in the lurch by intimating that he has tried to give them an objective account of Christian doctrine rather than of what he is sure that he himself believes. This seems to me a fine return of More upon himself, a crowning evidence of the unremitting veracity and humility of his spirit.

The truth is that from first to last he was in the main a Platonist, by constitution and by reason of the studies that occupied the greater part of his life. But in advanced middle age he saw very clearly that Platonism at its best (that is, as he knew it and lived by it) is a preparation for Chris-

[2] Princeton, 1934.   [3] New Haven, 1935.

tianity. Therefore he set himself—rather with head than with heart, I think, though by no means without heart—to show how Plato's doctrines found their completion eight centuries later in the dogmas of the Catholic Christian Church, especially in the pronouncements of the Council of Chalcedon. He confessed to friends that early in life he had found himself confronted by a sharp dilemma: Christ must be either a madman or a god. (This dilemma is a normal one for the academic reason, a point that will be dwelt upon in a later chapter.) And now he decided that Christ must be God; that otherwise there was no reality in Plato's difficult doctrine of Ideas, wherein there is assumed an inexplicable union of the divine and the human; a union unbelievable if it could never be historic and personal and complete.

So far, so good. But it is one thing to believe that Jesus Christ is both God and man in a unique sense; quite another thing to believe that this unique sense can be defined with anything like adequacy by the human reason, or that the reason's efforts in this direction are of anything like prime importance. We cannot even be sure, without presumption, that the word "Incarnation" itself is a permanent fixture. It is impregnated with the implications of the Latinistic stage of occidental civilization; and in some future religious era there may become current a more suitable term to denote the supreme historical fact that occasioned the dogma. Christology is not an exact science; and at present, like the science of the atom, it is in a marked state of transition. A number of contemporary and authoritative religious thinkers have adopted in this field a far more tentative tone than More's. Search, for instance, the writings of Von Hügel and A. E. Taylor, or even the more decisive utterances of William Temple (Archbishop of York), noting what they say, or refrain from saying, on the subject of Christology; then place your findings alongside the definitions given by More. The difference is very significant. I recall a characteristic passage in which the late Baron von Hügel, that great Roman Catholic saint of the intellect, remarks that the revelation of God in Jesus Christ "is in *some* sense unique" (italics mine). But More set himself to define that sense as precisely as he could.

In *The Skeptical Approach* he says that in Christ divine revelation is of "a new *form* . . . unique in *kind* as well as in degree" [4] (italics mine). All previous prophets and teachers, though they prepared the way for Christ, must be placed in an essentially different category. As for ordinary religious persons: "We may speak of being in God, but it is only by a loose and rather dangerous metaphor that we may speak of God being in us. Man's reason and conscience may be divine, they are not the indwelling of divinity." In fact, the scale of divine revelation "is *not continuous* but interrupted at least at three points in the ascending passage from inanimate to animate, from animal to man, and from the dualism of man to the dualism of the God-man." This comes perilously near to claiming that, by constitution, Jesus is as different from man as man is from the animals.

But More, shrinking back (I think) from that gulf, hastens to assure us that our human faith in divine revelation is, unlike that revelation itself, entirely "*continuous*," evincing "no break, no distinction in kind." For if such were not the case (though More does not state this point) Jesus Christ's faith in God would be of a different *kind* from other men's faith in God; which would be an inhuman paradox. So, according to More, our faith in the Divine Being, whether

[4] See pp. 163 ff.

He is revealed through Jesus or through other men, is a single kind of faith—though the revelation through Jesus is different in kind from the revelation through other men! Here is an intolerable dichotomy of revelation and faith. Later More says that "Christianity alone of religions corresponds with the final data of self-knowledge." [5] But surely our final datum is the indwellingness of the divine will, of transcendent deity; and our knowledge of that, if we follow out More's logic, must be different in *kind* from Christ's knowledge of it. Thus we come to the gulf that More would fain avoid: the inmost experience of the knowing, praying, believing, loving, and serving Jesus of Nazareth is different from ours in *kind*. If so, we cannot really take part in his experience.

The gentle reader may justifiably exclaim, "Oh, what a tangled web we weave when the warp of our Christological pattern is the word *kind!*" Would not the words "quality" and "possession" be somewhat less objectionable? Consider what happens when a great poet expresses an old human emotion or idea with perfect originality, with original perfection. "The quality of mercy is not strained. . . ." Or, "Tomorrow and tomorrow and tomorrow. . . ." Those two experiences are as old as the human race. But Shakespeare, for the moment entirely possessed by them, is possessed also of the perfect words and tune for them. His experience is the same kind as ours but supreme in poetic quality and possession. In Christ men find the same kind of life or being as their own; otherwise they could not really know it or share it. But in Him it has unique perfection of quality: his will is completely possessed by and of the Divine Will. And this complete possession is sublimely, divinely, different from the incomplete possession that we

[5] P. 178.

find in other persons, no matter of how high a quality their lives may be, for instance, the Buddha. We say, with a certain rightness, of a supreme passage of verse, "This is infinitely better than any other passage on the same subject." And when we compare the most Christlike life that we know with the Life of Christ, we say with entire rightness, "This is infinitely better." Here indeed the light that lighteth every man, the Word that creates all things, becomes flesh and dwells among us (and we behold his glory, glory as of the only begotten of the Father) full of grace and truth. . . . One is driven to quote St. John because one's own words are so weak and fumbling. My point is that the words "quality" and "possession" are somewhat less objectionable than the word "kind" as employed by More. They seem to me closer to the sense of the New Testament, and to the trend of the most authoritative Christological thinking of the present time in so far as I have studied it. More's system, I am sure, is not highly authoritative. And if, as Professor Shafer complains, More himself does not entirely believe it, so much the better. For, I must say, in the upshot, it is unbelievable.

Also I think that More's Christologic system weakens the force of his earlier dualistic philosophy, considered in the first part of this essay. As Christologist he urges that the duality of the nature of Jesus is "*analogous* [my italics] to the duality of the supernatural and the natural in man, but it is different also [the context shows he means different in kind] in being the duality of divinity and humanity." This thought, as More develops it, seems to me to mean that, except in the case of Christ, there is no *real* reality, so to speak, in the commingling of the divine and human in human life. When, for instance, Sir Philip Sidney prays, "Eternal Love, maintain thy life in me," the words "thy

life" do not or should not really mean that. They do not
even mean "a life which is an image of thy life"; for an
image may really partake of that which it images. The right
meaning according to More's logic must be "a life which is
analogous to thy life." And therefore that "true universal
in human nature" exalted by More as Platonist [6] is not truly
universal: it is merely an analogue of the Universal Life.
There can be no essential correspondence between two
things that are merely analogous. Here again poetry may
help us. The Roman Catholic martyr, Robert Southwell,
wrote:

> Man's soul of endless beauty image is,
> Drawn by the work of endless skill and might. . . .

Southwell knew that the Universal Artist puts himself
really, though inexplicably, into the image that he creates.

The truth is that the main significance of More's Christian thought lies in its strong critical reaction against that
religious humanitarianism which, enthroning nature in
place of God, reduces Christ to "a mere man," as the
phrase goes. At the same time (this point will be developed in the fifth chapter) he was reacting from the non-
theological humanism of Irving Babbitt, which More's own
outlook had formerly approximated but which, he now believed, could provide no ultimate defense against humanitarian assaults. Those two reactions drove him into a kind
of Christological absolutism—despite his brilliant and effectual denunciations of the "Demon of the Absolute" in
other fields of thought.

Milton, I believe, had continually to fight the devil of
pride in his own breast and was therefore able in his chief

[6] See above, p. 55.

poem to make the character of Satan extraordinarily vivid and appealing. Similarly More could powerfully sketch and confute the Demon of the Absolute because this very creature was always trying to ensnare him. Witness his relentless criticism of the Absolute in German philosophy and of the absolutist tendency which he found in Roman Catholic theology; both are dealt with in his penetrating essay on Von Hügel. More could not believe in a God whose will is absolutely law. "I must attribute the evil of the world," he says, "to some other obscurely guessed factor that thwarts the full working of His will . . . there is something in the sum of existence besides the will of God, and beyond that patent fact I deem it folly to conjecture." [7] This utterance, whether or no it be theologically correct, is humanly appealing, and it stands in remarkable contrast to his reasonings about Christ. Those reasonings are not supported, I believe, by the Synoptic Gospels; therefore More terms these, in a misfortunate passage, "the humanitarian gospels." That adjective, when we consider the connotations given to it by More's total work, simply will not do; it does not apply to those three sublimely human versions of the life of Christ. Here More's thought is gored by the horn of the Demon of the Absolute. In short, my impression is that, over against the age-old absolutism of metaphysics, More's thinking tends to humanize the idea of God; but that, because of his extreme though valuable reaction against the new humanitarianism, his logic tends to dehumanize Christ.

However, when a person remarked to me recently that More's books "smell of the lamp," I exclaimed, "But what a lamp!" A clear and steady light, continually noble, pervades the reaches of his immense scholarship. And it is always a challenging and educative light. The reader may

[7] *Skeptical Approach*, pp. 163-64.

often differ from the author's ideas but not, unless he is a far too gentle reader, without a real effort to clarify his own. At the same time the reader may feel that More's ideas upon the highest matters suffer from a certain deficiency of the poetic spirit. This spirit by itself cannot give us the highest truth, but without it the highest truth is not given. More lacks the lumination of an Emerson; whom, as he liked to say, he adored this side of idolatry. Let us then place More in our bookcase a little lower than that angel; but not too far away. He is the necessary complement and corrective to Emerson. The light of that great but confused sage has burned muddily in a thousand subsequent writers. More brought to the scene the cleansing light of a great critical intellect. . . . Emerson sometimes gives us the impression that he had a feeling that, in his own light, he had caught up with Jesus. More, after long and severe searchings for high truth, placed his lamp, in his own way, at the feet of the glory of Christ.

4.

Stuart Sherman and the War Age

THAT HOUR IN THE END OF AUGUST, 1926, WHEN THE news of Sherman's death reached me is marked in my memory with a kind of black silence. It recalls the strange quiet that fell upon the American scene a few years earlier when the robust voice of Theodore Roosevelt ended. But Sherman was in mid-career; he had not reached his forty-fifth birthday. Ahead of him, one hoped, were the years in which so versatile an essayist might win a fuller maturity. In the previous year I had taken part in extending to him the invitation of Bowdoin College to be one of the speakers in her institute of contemporary American literature. The occasion was in tune with his latest affiliations and he expressed a keen interest in it. But finally he declined the invitation on the ground that he was overwhelmed, yet happily overwhelmed, he intimated, with his new duties as editor of *Books*. And now it is clear from his *Life* [1] that he was joyously and unwittingly working himself to death. During his summer vacation in 1925 he was restless for New York. "I shall be very happy to return and have a regular job on my hands all the time, with no margin for meditation between." And later: "Since I have left the sure academic treadmill which keeps one in motion with

[1] Jacob Zeitlin and Homer Woodbridge, *Life and Letters of Stuart P. Sherman*, New York, 1929.

no commotion, I find an increasing craving for stimulus."
Such was his mood in his last year. Never till this year, so
he remarked with democratic jocularity, had he had "a
really heart-filling sense of life as one damned thing after
another." Heart-filling but also heart-breaking. Four
months after this remark, without any warning that Sherman would heed, his overstrained heart suddenly gave way.

Yet the mood of his last months is quite characteristic of
his life as a whole. The consistency of his *temperament* appears from first to last in the *Life*. This fascinating though
in some important respects too uncritical book, by two devoted and competent friends of Sherman, seems to me of
equal value with his essays. For he was more distinguished
as a person than as a critic. Though I had read his critical
works with pleasure, I was never tempted to reread them
with care, until this biography sent me eagerly back to
them. They lack that originative depth of meditation
which in the most compelling books of criticism, like the
continual voice of an underground stream, lures the reader
to retrace his steps thoughtfully, again and again. But now
I find in them one voice of a many-toned personality that
needed to express itself in many ways: in multitudinous
daily labors, in snatches of sport and pastime and travel, in
keen words and baffling silences among his friends, in hasty
notebook jottings and, best of all, in a voluminous and
vivid correspondence with an extraordinary variety of ac-
quaintances.

If his *Life* be read along with his works the whole forms
a singular picture of the literary and educational life of
America during the quarter century centering in the World
War. No other writer so fully embodied the strange antith-
eses of that period. An American wit has remarked that
Sherman "tried to combine in himself the two Babbitts"—

Professor Irving Babbitt and the George F. Babbitt of Sinclair Lewis's novel *Main Street*.

His unsteadiness in the war period was due to the paradoxicalness of the age, added to his own. The *Life* says he was "vivid, austere, playful, serious, tempery, suave, humorous, sardonic, gentle, severe, passionate, stoical, egotistic, generous, poetic, rational." This engaging list rightly omits the word "grave." Sherman was deficient in a certain kind of gravity, hard to define, which is central in the critical nature. The authors of the *Life* are also right in asserting that "the fundamental trait of Sherman's criticism, underlying all his attitudes and principles, is a splendid gusto, a huge enjoyment of many kinds of literary excellence." But they are wrong in their feeling, expressed at the close, "that he was destined to attain to a profounder synthesis of the critical spirit than anyone had yet reached in America." For they have demonstrated to the reader in eight hundred pages that Sherman lacked the necessary gravity for such a profound synthesis, and that he lacked the necessary condition for such a gravity. The necessary condition is not a splendid gusto underlying all the critic's principles. It is a firm set of principles underlying all his splendid gusto.

Sherman's insecurity and inconsequence in respect to critical principles were partly the cause and partly the result of his extraordinary impressibility. This feature of his temperament was concealed by his attitude of complete independence—a sincere attitude which, like Theodore Roosevelt's, was derived from democratic modernity and buttressed by a sturdy moral character. Near the end of the *Life* it is hinted that Sherman was not apt at making a "serious apology" for a past deed or utterance. But also he was very inapt at confessing and scrutinizing the influences exerted upon him by other persons. An intensely social being, he was keenly though hiddenly susceptible to personal pressures. Time and again one finds him imperturbably waiving the advice of others, only to discover, later on, that it has had a decided effect upon him. His impressibility is the main key, I think, to the paradox of his career: his early adoption and later abandonment of the aims of high criticism.

It was the personality rather than the ideas of Professor Babbitt that captured Sherman as a graduate student in Harvard University. His predisposition was for poetic gusto, not for consistent thought. Son of a wandering Yankee, he had had an irregular, impecunious and quite adventurous boyhood in the Middle and Far West. As a youth of thirteen, roughcut and prematurely responsible, he came to his ancestral Vermont with a feeling of awkward disdain for the East and with no ambition to attend college, much less to become what he later delighted to call a "damned professor," although deeper still in his nature was a love of sound conventions. In Williams College he displayed the ineptitude of the average undergraduate in regard to ideas. But he continued and developed the poetic zest for reading and for writing that had been awakened in him by a teacher in his last year in high school, when he had galloped through Jowett's *Plato*, Spenser, and the Romantic poets "in search of the gusto I heard in that teacher's voice, in search of the glow I had seen in that teacher's eyes." His experience with Professor Babbitt was similar.

Certain others of Babbitt's pupils, put on their guard by the ruthlessness of his pursuit of great ethical ideas, have managed to hold his thought at arm's length and to attain in middle age a somewhat critical view of it suited to their own capacities. Sherman's procedure was just the other way around. He embraced Babbitt's philosophy immedi-

ately, externally, and statically. He was captivated by Babbitt's work not primarily as an avenue to truth but as the
literary expression of a vigorous and distinguished personality. He imitated the ways of Babbitt and also of Paul E.
More in his yearning for literary self-expression. He could
imitate them with remarkable success just because of his
acute impressibility, and because in combination with native literary genius he had a certain intellectual simplicity.
The ideas of his two masters did not penetrate him deeply
but sprang up quickly like the seed that fell on stony
ground.

The resulting book, *On Contemporary Literature*
(1917), has in it a note of quick and hard brilliance. Yet it
is not only a rare production for a critic in his early thirties,
it is one of the really distinguished works of criticism in
our language. In the opening chapter, how warmly the
democracy of Mark Twain is felt and how simply its limitation is seen: "Twain does not give us much help toward
realizing our best selves; but he is a rock of refuge when
the ordinary self, the 'divine average,' is in danger"! The
ensuing chapters on leading current novelists show that
"ordinary self" endangered by abnormal selves masquerad-
ing as supernormal selves, in the cloak of esthetic naturalism. With the suavest yet exactest irony the masks are
twitched off; especially in the most finished and satisfying
essay of all, the one on George Moore. No wonder this
gentleman found the book the "ugliest" he had ever read. It
is the effectual opponent of enamelled nastiness: it is wholesome, militant, bright-smiling good sense. Heaven knows—
what George Moore was too knowing to know—how much
the time needed it and how much the times will continue to
need it.

Sherman's enemies were mistaken, and his friends fatefully mistaken, in depreciating his first book as derivative and in regarding his second book, *Americans* (1922), as more fruitfully critical. The *Life* says: "In *Americans* there is a greater body of writing that should endure than in any other single book of Sherman's. Only the first two topics owe their being to a controversial impulse, while one or two others are of doubtful vitality. But the essays on Franklin, Emerson, Hawthorne, Whitman, Roosevelt, the Adamses, and Mr. Paul Elmer More are as solidly based as they are brilliantly written." And elsewhere: "Perhaps it is the most substantial of all his books. The studies are done with rare penetration and balance. . . . There are few books better fitted to give to Americans an understanding of the values of the national inheritance. To open and close this volume there are essays on Mr. Mencken and Mr. More which serve to define Sherman's position. He is perhaps not equally far from the Nietzschean individualism of Mencken and the reactionary humanism of More, but he is now remote from both; and his position, as compared with either extreme, is central."

This is a good example of bad American criticism. It is warm and amiable half-truth. It is fundamentally confused. It is typical of that American academic outlook with which Sherman's friends wrongly identified the thought of More and Babbitt, and from which they wrongly fancied that Sherman was now freeing himself. It is the sort of criticism that Sherman himself was being influenced to write and to be satisfied with.

Many of the world's best critical writings, perhaps most of them, have "owed their being to a controversial impulse." Controversy is the natural pabulum of good criticism, and the critic should offer up thanks for it as for his daily bread. Why, then, is *Americans* praised for being almost devoid of it? Because the academic mind dislikes "controversial impulse" and looks askance upon the battle of radically opposed principles; and because in America this aversion has been abnormally heightened by the genial influence of Emerson and Whitman which, stiffly resisted at first, has gradually succeeded in seeping throughout our academe. By the second decade of the twentieth century American literary academics had become shyly but surely in love with the romantic, soaring, tolerant, vague and uncritical idealism of the previous century. Therefore it was disconcerting to be abruptly summoned by More and Babbitt, presently assisted by the World War, to an austere overhauling of that very idealism. We academics (I am speaking confessionally) felt like a middle-aged bachelor who, having long resisted the blandishments of a local beauty, leads her at last towards the altar, only to have his ears assailed by two stern voices announcing just cause and impediment. We had always known that Romantic idealism was far from perfect, but we could not see how prostitute it had now become. The situation was most disconcerting; indeed it was hateful. As for the War, our hatred of that "controversial impulse" was restrained by our necessary public spirit and patriotism. All the better could we hate the war of ideas begun by those two violent "radicals," Babbitt and More.

The common supposition that the "radical" humanism of these two critics had for its chief opponent the naturistic radicalism of the journalists, and that the latter was mainly responsible for converting or perverting Sherman, is not tenable. Loud, to be sure, was the outcry of current writers against Babbitt and More. But, after all, the current writers were children howling in the night and with no language but a howl. On the other hand the opposition of the academics was not loud but deep. It was a fixed, blind, shrugging aversion; and it was effectual. It postponed for a generation or more any general understanding of the central truth of modern humanism. Only the academics had the requisite learning to understand that truth—and to misunderstand it. Their fault was not that they "criticized," but that they failed to *criticize*, Babbitt and More. These two writers, not fairly encountered on their own ground, remained unfought, unvalued. They are more faulty, and far more significant, than the American academic mind has so far succeeded in perceiving. This imperception came to be Sherman's also.

Like President Wilson, whom he revered, Sherman was an animated academic conservative molded by nineteenth-century idealism. Like Theodore Roosevelt, to be sure, he had a fighting style and he complained that "professors won't fight." But like his brother professors he became averse from the combat of essential principles. Immensely shocked by the World War, he felt intensely and mistakenly that democracy is an essential principle. Therefore unlike his two masters he missed the root meaning of the World War and helped his countrymen to miss it. He did not face the root evils of modern civilization. He was not a radical thinker any more than he was ever a radical emotionalist. In an age of intense inner conflicts he had none. The mental and moral *Sturm und Drang* of the era never went beneath his surface even in the unsettled days of his youth. He accepted with healthy simplicity the *mores* he inherited from New England. He accepted them as the natural and necessary bases of his own personality. So far from rebelling against them, as others were doing, he never really questioned them. Nor on the other hand did he cut beneath them, as Babbitt and More were doing, into a deeper and more cosmopolitan ethic. What he did was to modify or mollify his New England *mores* in the light of what he learned from Franklin, Whitman, Arnold, Pater, Meredith and Stevenson. For these writers, along with Hawthorne and Emerson, he had a warm and old-fashioned devotion. In brief, he was a late, brilliant, academic devotee of nineteenth-century idealism, particularly in its American form and with Emerson as its central luminary.

Hence his second volume, *Americans*. In a certain academic sense it is indeed, as Professors Zeitlin and Woodbridge say, "substantial." But in the critical sense it is not "solidly based" nor has it "rare penetration," for its critical outlook is obsolete at a number of crucial points. Otherwise it is an excellent introduction to American literature and tradition. It is a series of clear, vigorous, and devoted expositions. But on the whole it is textbooky. Its style lacks the fine irony that fascinates the reader in the best of Sherman's writings and that constituted one of his main charms as a man among men. His personal charm is admirably brought out in the *Life*. Why did the authors not feel the lack of it in *Americans*? Because in approaching this volume they submerged their critical sense—as Sherman himself had done.

He did so preëminently in approaching Emerson. His essay on Emerson was "conceived in the interest of the gospel of democracy, and he put more work into it than into anything of that length he had ever written." It has some excellent qualities; but in the upshot it is hopelessly naïve. After reading it one feels the need of recurring to C. E. Norton's treatment of the same subject in his *Letters*, which had appeared ten years earlier. Norton loved Emerson and fully appreciated his greatness as an American writer. Yet in the end he found him "the most innocent, the most inexperienced of men who have lived in and reflected on the world . . . he is not one of the universal men in a large sense, but a man of some universal sympathies and relations curiously and instructively hampered by local, provincial bonds." This is precisely the point at which Emerson must be discounted if the authority of his noble qualities is to be maintained for the more sophisticated and cosmopolitan America of the twentieth century. But in the face of this new America, and indeed for its very sake, Sherman tried to maintain entire the ideally universal Emerson who continued to flourish in the late-Romantic academic mind. Sherman was discipular of the Emersonian naïveté and happy confusion. Therefore one need not be surprised to find him a little later (in his essay on W. C. Brownell) praising Norton and quoting from him with approval this sentence on Emerson: "He was the friend and helper of America's youth; but for the difficulties and struggles of its manhood *we need the wisdom of the reflective and rational understanding,* not that of the intuitions." The italics are Sherman's. He did not pause to reflect that he was here bringing in a witness against his own essay on Emerson. Why bother about consistency? Emerson did not.

The opening and closing pieces in *Americans,* which serve, says the *Life,* "to define Sherman's central position," miss fire just because his central position was now so shaky. Both are clever but neither is clever enough. In ultimate tone the skit on Mencken is sputtery and the one on More is falsetto. Neither journalistic radicalism nor "radical" humanism could be daffed aside so easily as Sherman had come to fancy. Mencken was the symbol of a more valid discontent with the American "Nordic" tradition than Sherman perceived. As for More, Sherman here urged him to discover that "the average man is, like himself, at heart a mystic, vaguely hungering for a peace that diplomatists cannot give, obscurely seeking the permanent amid the transitory." But More was already acquainted with that fact. The real question at issue was, and is, this: how may *criticism* best proceed to clear the way for the average man toward that true peace, that sense of permanence amid the transitory? Sherman's proposal, in the same paragraph, is that the critic should become more warmly aware of the virtues of the average man and of the "religion of democracy." This is good nineteenth-century doctrine. Even diplomatists have now accepted it. But it has proved entirely inadequate precisely as a means of bringing to the average man "the peace that diplomatists cannot give."

Paul E. More, on the other hand, had been proposing in his writings that those who influence the average man, the leaders of opinion, should severely revise and deepen their own moral ideas. Sherman was right in the preface of his first volume when he called More "one of the most penetrating moralists of our times" and approved, with proper reservations, his epigram on Goethe's *Faust*. Commenting upon Goethe's representation of the devil as the spirit that denies, More had declared that the spirit that denies is God. "I do not recall any single utterance from living lips," wrote Sherman, "that has impressed me as more profoundly illuminating." Well, if he had thought this matter through he would have decided that Emerson to a considerable extent, and democracy to a very great extent, had discarded the God who denies; and that there could be no firm way of Peace for the average man until his leaders had rediscovered this aspect of deity, this restrictive and humbling function of the spiritual Will.

However, I cannot find that, after his first fine careless rapture, Sherman gave this matter any serious attention.

More's "profoundly illuminating" epigram could not have illuminated him very profoundly. The gleam was doused, I think, by the tide of general approval that met the position he assumed in *Americans*. Accepting the general feeling that More and Babbitt were "too negative," he lost his former conviction that their Nay was not ultimately devilish. "In their ultimate position," he wrote in a hot and revealing letter of January 13, 1923, "they are both dogmatic and mystical, to an extent that makes it impossible for one to understand or follow them, to say nothing of expounding them." This is a valid confession. The "ultimate position" here alluded to is a very old one and has often been followed and expounded. But Sherman did not grapple with it steadily, in the writings either of Babbitt and More or of earlier and more genial humanists, such as Plato, Spenser, and Arnold, whom he admired. It is finally clear from the *Life* that he moved further and further away from a grave study of humanism.

What moved him, he thought, was the call of democratic America. In the crucial letter quoted above he rightly declared: "There is no question at the present time requiring more thinking, calling for a more definite stand, and demanding more *explicit* expression from the man of letters than precisely the question: What does democracy mean to me? A failure to deal honestly and intelligently with that question strikes me as a failure at pretty nearly the most important task of critical leadership." In the following year appeared Babbitt's *Democracy and Leadership*. This book has serious faults, but also it has precisely the qualifications enumerated by Sherman above. One finds him reading it in a period of quite exceptional leisure, during a voyage to England after resigning from the University of Illinois and before taking up his editorial duties in New York. But one does not find any significant reflections on his part, then or later, either for or against it. A reflective reader who has at heart the best interests of America should turn to Babbitt's chapter on "Democracy and Standards" and pause upon the passage beginning, "We come here to another opposition that is one of first principles and is therefore not subject to mediation or compromise—the opposition between the doctrine of the saving remnant and that of the divine average." Then he should read Sherman's almost contemporary essay, "Towards an American Type." Here the opposed doctrines of the "saving remnant" and the "divine average" are effectually confused. In the closing passage the confusion becomes damnable in a cheap and false parallel of St. Paul's "altar to the unknown God" with the "thronged altar" of present American democracy.

Elsewhere, in the course of one of his delightful attacks on Eastern American snobbery, Sherman asserts, "I do not believe in the saving remnant unless it is saving." Properly, I think, the term "saving-remnant" should be written as a noun with a hyphen in its middle; in which case the above witticism would be equivalent to saying, "I do not believe in an oak-tree unless it is an oak-tree." This is a sound credo. But the believer, especially if he happens to be a very gifted and influential critic, should proceed to clear his mind as to the qualities denoted by "oak" and the activities implied by "saving." Sherman omitted such clarification. Therefore with an easy conscience and a pleasant zest he was able to write *My Dear Cornelia*. This popular book, a reed rather than an oak, takes a hand in damning, I think, rather than in saving the democratic culture of America. For instance, the author's most explicit idea in regard to Prohibition seems to be that in a nation devoted to automobiling, drunkenness is too dangerous. Very true. But in a

nation devoted to democracy, the most fearful danger is
the mental and moral dishonesty exhibited by Prohibition.
This fact should surely have been insisted upon by the author, as a saving member of the saving-remnant. In general,
Sherman did not fulfill with entire accuracy his own pre-
scription.

My Dear Cornelia was written for the *Atlantic Monthly*.
Of late this journal has relinquished to other journals that
intellectual leadership in America which it once held. But
it has not done this overtly. It has endeavored, if I may
again cite a useful epigram, "to combine within itself the
two Babbitts." A magazine may cater legitimately to both
the few and the many if it overtly offers different levels of
value in its contents. But generally speaking the *Atlantic* of
the twentieth century has sought a single level. It has
wished to appeal to the saving-remnant and to all the sheep
of the house of Israel in one and the same idiom. It has
wished the sheep to feel, without changing their customary
and easy posture, that they too are shepherds. Thus has
arisen that pleasant prodigy known as "the *Atlantic* style."
A juster name might be "the Atlantic-and-Pacific style." It
is too smart for homely strength and too simple for strong
distinction. Well, in Sherman's *Life* one watches with a
horrid fascination the gradual drawing together of him and
the *Atlantic*. The influence of the editor, Mr. Sedgwick,
grows strong upon the impressible critic. "In their outlook
upon the American scene," we are told, "the two men saw
almost eye to eye. Both were in sympathy with democratic
forces and both desired to preserve an aristocratic principle
of taste within the democracy." Doubtless it was this principle of taste that shaped the culminating passage on religion in *My Dear Cornelia:* "Then I said, with my ultimate
effort: Cornelia, when one goes out at the church door, one

enters the universe. The only blessed mood that I know, comes when I feel that all the universe is holy." And so on.

However, *Cornelia* had no sequel, though the *Atlantic* kept wooing Sherman to produce one. It is happily clear that he soon became subconsciously dissatisfied with the milk-and-cinnamon manner of aristo-democracy. The select mediocrity of decadent Bostonese was crowded out of his affections by the mediocre selectness of literary New York. Moreover, the growing influence upon him of W. C. Brownell was tonic, though not exactly curative, for his taste. His delightful letters to his new patron are perhaps the most striking example of Sherman's tendency to adopt unwittingly the very idiom of a correspondent who interested and influenced him. Unfortunately the mood of diffusive tolerance that mastered Brownell in his closing years had the effect of reconfirming the younger critic in his academic democratism. But the fact is that Sherman did not take this doctrine quite so seriously as he thought he did. His attitude toward American equalitarianism resembled that of Disraeli toward British Toryism, so admirably noted by Sherman: "The inexhaustible fun which Disraeli offers to the student consists in contrasting the nervous, subtle, highly civilized intellectual that he was with the representative English country gentleman that he affected to be." Sherman was not affected. He could be simply sincere because he was so very deficient in critical self-survey. Yet his later writings offer to a sympathetic and discerning reader the sort of fun suggested above—the fun of contrasting the representative democrat that Sherman thought he wanted to be with the brilliant Protean essayist that he actually was.

It seems that he was in the main a personal rather than a critical essayist. And his later works, *Genius of America,*

Points of View, The Main Stream, Critical Woodcuts,
though lacking the concentration of *Americans,* are on the
whole better literature. They have far more personal distinction. They gave free play to his ranging moods and
observations, and to his rare gift for the dramatic etching
of diverse personalities. Wherever his writing has real distinction, this is due to the personal freshness, so to speak, of
his common sense and comic vision. For instance, in the
quietly devastating sketch of Samuel Butler, who was "far
more learned than any other English author in the psychology of impiety." Or in the bland moralizing of the address
on "Vocation," wherein the worn ideal of "service to mankind" is reformed in a slyly wholesome fashion. Or in the
laughing observations "On Falling in Love" and "On Falling in Hate," where it appears that the real theme of the
typical midwestern novel of free love is free hate. Or in
the happy essay on "Literature and the Government of
Men," where our current fear of "the *dead* hand of the
past" is rendered absurdly superstitious, and American democratism is subordinated (ah, Sherman!) to the "natural
and entirely free aristocracy of letters where no man has
any power whatever but the power of his own spirit upon
other spirits."

Ever and anon, to be sure, a soft ninth wave of vague
humanitarian sympathy swamps the critic's good sense. For
example, in his essays on Sherwood Anderson, D. H. Lawrence, and Willa Cather, which he placed with curious in-
discretion at the beginning of *Critical Woodcuts*—perhaps
to ingratiate current readers by showing them at the outset
how much in tune he could be with current writers. The
result is that the reader, unless permanently "current," is
tempted to drop the book at the beginning. For here the
critic's judgment is vacillating, his comic vision muddy and

his style dull. Not dull, however, is the opening passage on
D. H. Lawrence—"a shag of hair across the forehead, eyes
alert, defiant, glinting like a squirrel's, snubby nose sniffing
the air, and a big bush of a beard . . . worn out of reverence
for the Dark Gods which inhabit the Dark Forest of one's
own being." Let the reader therefore take heart of grace
and persist for eighty pages. Then he will come across a
luminous exposition of how H. G. Wells in his youth was
influenced to adopt a biased view of life: "Mid-Victorian
society, as the young Wells envisaged it, gazing from somewhere not far from its lower stratum, was a substance in
which he seemed to be fixed like a fly at the bottom of a
pan of cold mutton tallow." Here the reader is won; and
no subsequent wave of *warm* tallow (Shermanly speaking)
can entirely frizzle his interest in the book. In the admirable
essay on Boswell the reader will feel like applying to the
critic himself his encomium of Boswell's art: "he has a most
extraordinary faculty for taking in and giving forth again
all the elements in a situation which constitute its life." In
general, Sherman's latest writings are graphic appendices
to his distinguished book of criticism, *On Contemporary
Literature*.

The fact emerging from his total career is that his native
ironic good sense, early reinforced as it was by the influence of Babbitt and More, exerted a continual and creative
pullback upon the diffusive impressibility that he shared
with his contemporaries. Otherwise he would have disappeared head first into impressionism. He would perhaps
have fulfilled his recurrent desire to write novels, and no
doubt they would have been even less memorable than the
average effusion of the time. He perused a vast mass of current fiction with unflagging gusto. He read and *reread* H.
G. Wells! Greater love for his time hath no man than this.

Indeed, the passing day engaged the real chivalry that was prominent in Sherman's nature. As a boy of twelve, near to death from thirst in the Arizona desert, he gave his last share of water to save the life of an infant. As a man of forty, he devoted his latest energies to the appreciation of an infantile literature; and in a way he saved its life. Much of it will continue to live only in his essays upon it, and because he interpreted it in the light of a broad, healthy spirit. He salted much perishable stuff with his inimitable good spirits and sharp friendly irony. The most significant irony of the situation is this: a whole menagerie of current writers, confined to a small round of decadent notions and devoted to the sensation of a dismal vitality, snarling at everything normal, cheerful, or established, came in the end to lick the hand of a joyous academic apostle of common sense. Sherman fully earned the acclamations that came to him from the diverse American camps of the War Age. He showed his contemporaries a vitality of common sense that they had openly disdained but secretly needed. And thus he became the most representative American prose writer of the time. The others were too far gone in impressionism to make a representative impression. He, while his temperament was warmly engaged in the passing show, stood back a little with his mind and gave the thing some envisagement and meaning—at best, a comic meaning. He was able to do this because of his sound character and his humanistic training.

He could not dispel the firm ground-lines that his two early masters had given to his outlook, though he could not or did not (God knows which) build at once firmly and originatively upon them. Hence, in his last years, his half-confessed sense of essential confusion; and hence too, I think, his heightened desire to have "no margin for meditation" between his killing labors. The vague hybrid which he termed "democratic humanism," and which he loved or tried to love enthusiastically, blinded him to the fact that humanism can never give effectual aid to democracy unless it maintains its own proper distinction; that it has been fearfully undermined precisely by democratic forces; and that it cannot be re-established except by a radical revival of its essential doctrines. These doctrines are ignored, damned, or misinterpreted by the numerous post-Protestants and pseudoscientific humanitarians who, since Sherman's death, have proclaimed themselves humanists. Chains of so-called humanistic cults have extended themselves from one end of America to the other. Well, this is "democratic humanism"! Sherman helped to father it; but I think that his best spirit disclaims it. The plain truth is that humanism *for the sake of* democracy has to be, not a democratic humanism, but a radically real humanism. In his hapless essay on "The Point of View in American Criticism" (1922), Sherman advocates a "redintegration of the national will on the basis of a genuinely democratic humanism, recognizing as its central principle the duty of bringing the whole body of the people to the fullest and fairest human life of which they are capable." The duty recognized in the closing words is great, obvious, and perennial—for aristocrats and for democrats alike. But how is it to be fulfilled in twentieth-century America? How is a humane "redintegration of the national will" to be effected? Earlier in the same curious essay the right answer is suggested. The educated members of "the younger generation" must find the way, and lead the way, to a genuinely human happiness. They must find and accept its proper bounds and bonds. "What they deeply crave," says Sherman, "is a binding generalization of philosophy or religion or morals which will give direction and purpose, which will give channel and speed, to the languid diffusive drift of their lives." It is exactly this sort of "binding generalization" that Sherman failed to find; that "democratic humanism" is too shallow to afford; and that real humanism, letting the world go by, must laboriously try to build.

5.

On Religion and Humanism

§I

A Catholic View

IN TWO PREVIOUS CHAPTERS I HAVE SKETCHED BABBITT'S personality and More's philosophy. Consideration of Babbitt's philosophy will occupy much of this chapter, the main purpose of which is to assemble the ideas of Babbitt, of More, and of certain other persons (including, incidentally, myself) upon the difficult subject of the relation between humanism and religion. I can best open the subject by quoting from a letter written to me by Babbitt on September 15, 1919. The letter belongs to the earlier days of our acquaintance. It is one of Babbitt's many attempts to formulate his ideas upon the religious bearings of his humanism. But it has a peculiar value in that it was written in a nonpolemical vein to a fairly young man who, seeking light, could not be entirely satisfied with Babbitt's light. Note, too, that it was written some years before Babbitt's reflections on the matter in hand became somewhat exacerbated by his disapproval of More's growing theological trend.

"The paradox of the whole matter," he wrote, "is this: a philosophy of the 'inner check' when put theoretically and in terms of the intellect seems intolerably negative. But when this philosophy is actually *lived*, when it becomes innate in a personality, the inner check is then felt, not as something negative, but as a positive driving-power. This

is only another way of saying that the key to life is found
not in the intellect but in the will. For another name for
the inner check is the supernatural will or will to peace in
contradiction to man's ordinary will, which, in its most important aspect, may be defined as the will to power. Humanism does not go much beyond the effort to uplift and
purify and moderate man's ordinary self. But even here it
is strictly correct to use the word 'conversion'; for the
standard or centre with reference to which the moderating
is done lies in an opposite direction from man's outward
striving impulses. Since you quote Plato, reflect on the famous image of the 'cave' in the Republic.

"Religion, at least in its ultimate ambition, goes much beyond humanism; it enters at last into a region of pure peace,
'unshadowable in words,' that involves not merely a moderating of the ordinary self but a more or less complete
dying to it. The tremendous driving-power that one feels
behind the founder of Christianity is primarily the driving-
power, not of emotion (even sublimated emotion), but
of the supernatural will, the will to peace.

"What you crave at bottom is personality [i.e., divine
personality]; and this is a legitimate craving provided that
you are not led in satisfying it to make undue concessions
to the mere emotionalist. Some of your expressions would
seem to indicate that you incline in this direction—for example, your expression 'religious monism.' Genuine religion, above all genuine Christianity, is always sharply dualistic ('Who will deliver me from the body of this death,'
etc.). To be sure language is very treacherous in dealing
with these problems of the inner life. Thus you discriminate
sharply between 'inner check' and 'vital control'—terms that
for me are about synonymous. You may be interested, by
the way, to know that the Sanskrit term *antaryāmin* that

Colebrooke in his essay on the Vendanta rendered 'inward check'—a rendering that Emerson took from Colebrooke—means more literally 'inner guide' or 'controller'."

Certainly the kind of "humanism" defined in the first of those three paragraphs was "actually lived" by Babbitt himself; it became "innate in a personality" and was experienced "not as something negative but as a positive driving-power." The quotation as a whole will recall to the reader, I hope, the closing paragraphs of Chapter II, above. And it prepares the way for the finely catholic view of Babbitt's thought in Professor Mercier's recent book, *The Challenge of Humanism.*[1]

The central figure of this book is Irving Babbitt. A strange and, for many, a solemn quiet is left by the stilling of that battling voice; but now we should be able to hear its meaning more clearly than ever. For Babbitt, strenuous, polemical, and profound, was one of the least persuasive of writers; and it is fortunate that just at this time a critic so urbane as Mercier should have ready, after years of preparation, a volume that exhibits his colleague's thought against its proper background and in its true perspective. Mercier's treatment is extraordinary in its union of sympathetic insight and detachment. As a Roman Catholic, apparently quite orthodox, he cannot adopt Babbitt's position. But he believes that, so far as it goes, it is less assailable and more fruitful than the creed advanced by any other modern humanist.

After a long survey of Babbitt's challenge to naturism on historical grounds, Mercier devotes a chapter to a much needed clarification of the psychology inherent in his

[1] Louis A. Mercier, *The Challenge of Humanism,* an Essay in Comparative Criticism. New York, 1933.

works. The most fundamental of the misunderstandings regarding it, is "the failure to note that Babbitt is just as profoundly impressed as any naturist with the fact of 'the many,' of the stream of change in which man is living"; but he refuses to become dizzy and unbalanced in watching that stream. "To exaggerate the oneness of life [Mercier writes] and merge it into the All-One, until we lose the sense of individuality, is one extreme; to exaggerate the multiplicity of life, until we lose the sense of standards to which classes of objects should conform, the sense of a universal of which particulars are but variations, is the other. These are the two exaggerations between which naturalism has oscillated." In opposition to that extremism Babbitt asserts: "Life does not give here an element of oneness and there an element of change, but a oneness that is always changing." Man has therefore the task of discovering the abiding in and through the flux; and his main means of doing so is the "higher imagination." The ordinary imagination is apt to preoccupy itself with the flux, as it has done more and more during the past two centuries. Before it can make a reliable contact with "the permanent order" through and beyond the flux it must be disciplined by reason, informed by meditation on the wisdom of the ages, and, above all, lifted and purified by the "higher will."

"Here," says Mercier, "we come to the ultimate aspect of Irving Babbitt's doctrine, the most subtle, no doubt the most objectionable to his naturalistic critics, and the one which, on the other hand, arouses the suspicion of his Christian well-wishers." The author claims that Babbitt's treatment of the higher will has been misrepresented by even so acute a thinker as Dr. Fulton J. Sheen and by even so close a friend as Paul Elmer More. In his chapter on More, Mercier shows how natural has been the transition of that distinguished critic from his earlier views, in which his preoccupation with Platonic and Hindu ideas kept him aloof from Christianity, to his present position in which his Platonism reinforces his belief in the Christian revelation. More may now be called a Catholic Anglican. On this point Mercier remarks: "It is vain to propose to us membership in the Anglican Church, as Mr. More does, on the ground that it offers the kind of revelation which neither in book nor in Church is absolute but in both book and Church possesses a sufficient authority. Logically two imperfect authorities cannot give certitude, especially when each must get its authority from the other." However, More's view, if I understand it, is that a revelation coming from within the believer himself, in a way quite in harmony with Catholic thought, reinforces those two imperfect but sufficient authorities and provides a kind of "certitude" beyond which it is presumptuous in this world to aspire. The kind of "infallibility" which Mercier in the context attributes to the Roman Catholic Church belongs of right, many believe, to the Church Invisible. They believe that the Deity is too wise to place such a guarantee upon any earthly institution no matter how divinely inspired. Elsewhere Mercier condemns what may be called the divinization of the nation in modern times but fails to observe that one root of this was the medieval divinization of the Church.

From such questions one returns happily to Babbitt's doctrine of the higher will, which, as Mercier says, is at once "humanism and super-humanism" and has the great advantage, in these unsettled times, of providing a ground of spiritual agreement for persons of all creeds and races. By itself it cannot restore—here I agree with the author—but it can point us to "the dynamism of the Christian ages, the rapture of being delivered from time and place and of being in union for eternity with the whole spiritual world."

Mercier claims that Babbitt in isolating his "higher will" from theistic and revealed religion is true to the natural separation that exists between philosophy and theology, as recognized so notably by the medieval Scholastics. In their philosophy they studied man merely as a rational animal moved by natural volition; allocating to theology the subject of man's highest will, i.e., divine Grace. Babbitt regards the higher will in man as ultimately divine, as supernatural in the sense that it checks and controls our natural will and reason. But he establishes it merely as a datum of human consciousness, a "higher immediacy" no less "given" and demonstrable than the immediate clamor of our lower desires. Refusing to go into its metaphysical implications, he shows its supreme importance for human conduct and happiness.

It creates the "man of character," who by his example accomplishes for humanity a solid good that cannot be given by the finest theories and sentiments. The man of spiritual character, whether Christian or non-Christian, saint or citizen, is (in Mercier's words) "one who meditates so deeply on the fact of the higher will in him and concentrates so intensely,—intellectually and imaginatively,—on his own and the race's experience of it that he attains to religious insight." One might add, what Mercier's strictly impersonal method prevents him from doing, that Irving Babbitt himself was such a man and that his works, whatever their fate in other respects, will hold their place as the unconscious self-revelation of a great and helpful person.

§2

T. S. Eliot and Irving Babbitt

A proper task for a young scholar proceeding towards the degree of Doctor of Philosophy in Harvard University would be a dissertation upon "The Influence of Irving Babbitt on Thomas Stearns Eliot." Eliot was a student of Babbitt's at Harvard, and in conversation (so I am informed) has been heard to refer to him as "master," acknowledging a strong indebtedness. In *After Strange Gods*, published in 1934, where he places Babbitt among the modern "heretics" whom he deprecates, he nevertheless speaks of him as "one for whose memory I have the highest respect and admiration." But presently he remarks, rather nonplussingly, that Babbitt's name "instantly suggests that of Ezra Pound, his peer in cosmopolitanism." The word "peer" is dubious in this context. Babbitt's cosmopolitanism differs from Mr. Pound's in quality, I think—that is, in nature and in value— if not in quantity. The question of quantity would require an extensive investigation; which I must leave to the scholar proposed above. It would provide an illuminating appendix to his discussion of Babbitt's effect on Eliot.

But that effect—here I must warn the ambitious doctoral candidate—is mainly the kind that scholars term "indirect influence." It appears less when Eliot is speaking (in print, at least) directly of Babbitt than when he is dealing with other topics. For instance, in the volume named above, when considering Thomas Hardy, in whose outlook he rightly finds a real moral baseness, Eliot says: "If somewhat deficient in vitality, people imagine passion to be the surest sign of vitality. This in itself may go towards accounting for Hardy's popularity." Such a passage is in close accord with Babbitt's critical thought; and so is the following perception: "It is in moments of moral and spiritual struggle depending on spiritual sanctions, rather than in those bewildering minutes in which we are all very much alike, that men and women are nearest to being real." Of course I do not mean to detract from the originality, in the best sense of this word, of Eliot's ethical insight. Moreover that insight, since his conversion to Christianity, has no doubt been nourished by the explicitly Christian writers rather than by Babbitt. But in his formative years Eliot must have been affected by his Harvard master in a crucial manner, a manner that prepared him later on to enter the Christian Church with a strong moral as well as emotional conviction.

That fact seems to me written throughout Eliot's work in invisible ink. Perhaps it could be rendered visible as day by the acid of investigative literary science. May the young scholar to whom I am recommending that task bring a very sharp insight to bear on the text of Eliot's writings. Incidentally he might also interview Mr. Eliot in the flesh. Time was when the field of the Ph.D. dissertation was restricted to dead authors. But that rule has now been happily relaxed, even in Harvard, I believe; and Mr. Eliot is still, happily, very much alive. In spite of his known reserve he might be induced by a fresh and eager inquisitor from his Alma Mater to give valuable oral evidence in this case. It is an important case. It illustrates significantly the underground and seeping fashion of much of Babbitt's influence.

It has been pointed out that William Wordsworth had an abiding effect upon many subsequent writers who ostensibly broke with him. Babbitt's fate is similar. Antipodal as he was to Wordsworth he resembled him in rocklike individuality, in strong sense of mission and iterative tenacity of manner. Babbitt was not one of those teachers who, knowing how very much may be said on every side of a question, are primarily anxious to give full play to the budding minds of their students. He bent them forcibly towards his light. So that later on, in the process of finding their own form, they were apt by way of reaction to lean away from him extremely; that is, if they had a marked temperamental bent of their own. But if they had also a sufficient moral depth of soil, Babbitt's influence persisted in their roots and fibers; even while their posture, their formal position, was averted from his clamant kind of humanism.

Hence the remarkable vagary that appeared in the second phase (alas, the third and maturest phase, which many of us awaited, was prevented by death) of the critical writings of Stuart Sherman, one of Babbitt's most gifted pupils. And it seemed to me that the same consideration helped, at least, to account for the extreme position taken by T. S. Eliot in his article in *The Forum*, July, 1928, on "The Humanism of Irving Babbitt." I believed that after a while Mr. Eliot would wish to revise that essay in the direction of fairness and adequacy. But he has republished it twice without, I think, any essential alteration. It is included in his current volume, *Essays Ancient and Modern;* where, moreover, he refrains from reprinting two other early papers "with which" (he explains in the preface) "I was dissatisfied." Clearly, then, he is not yet dissatisfied by his dissatisfaction with Babbitt's humanism.

Eliot's truest instinct in this essay is that religion at its best surpasses humanism always—as Babbitt always admits. However, there are many different grades of religion and of humanism. Suppose we let grade M represent the common or barnyard variety of each. (I seem to be under the influence of the logical style of the doctoral dissertation, with which my thoughts were concerned above.) Grade M religion is flat institutionalism; grade M humanism is flat common sense. Precise statistics are not available but I should estimate that those two powers have been about equal, and equally necessary, in the story of human civilization. Common sense must ever take the temple with a grain of salt; whereas on the other hand the salt loseth its savor, in the end, without the temple. Institutional religion has a tendency to senselessness, but is properly, nevertheless, the chief base and organ of the common sense—which has to keep working to make good sense of institutional religion. Remembering all that we owe to good human common sense, we must declare that there is certainly such a thing as a humanistic habit: it is the state of mind of many persons in many places at many times.

When Eliot declares that "there is no humanistic habit: humanism is, I think, merely the state of mind of a few persons in a few places at a few times"—he is thinking of grade A humanism or, let's say, grades A, B, and C. And over against these exceptional outcroppings of humanity, he sets the total bulk of religion, grades A to Z. This is to compare a quality with a quantity. This is to weigh a handful of humanistic gamecocks against a whole barnyard of religious mixed fowl. Naturally the gamecocks kick the beam. As for grade A religion, it too is certainly not a "habit": it appears in just "a few persons in a few places at a few times."

In this matter, as in the matter of Babbitt's and Pound's cosmopolitanisms, we have to distinguish quality and quantity. In addition we have to distinguish the few and the many. Eliot is entirely right, I am sure, in urging that not only the many but also the few as part of the many have permanent need of the temple. (His word for it is "re-

ligion," but "temple" or "church" seems to me a less ambiguous term for that which he mainly means.) He is right
in claiming that, without this, society cannot have "a spiritual co-ordination," and that in this regard Babbitt's humanism is inadequate. But the following assertion, while pur-
porting to speak for all, for both the few and the many,
speaks for the many only: "It is not clear that Mr. Babbitt
has any other enthusiasm to offer except the enthusiasm for
being lifted out of one's merely rational self—by some enthusiasm." (That suggestive dash, which does not now appear in the essay, has been retained by me, with scholiastic
zeal, from the first edition.)

The many, certainly, do not have the steady enthusiasm
of justice, the divine power of justice beyond "one's merely
rational self," that runs through the writings of Irving Babbitt. The many cannot have his devotion to those sublime
ideas or "natures" of truth, fortitude, and righteousness
which, as Emerson said, "no man ever gets above." Indeed
the very word "enthusiasm" in its old high meaning, which
Babbitt did so much to revive, is a repellent enigma to the
modern romantic mob, which (to apply here Eliot's words
regarding Babbitt) has no other enthusiasm except the enthusiasm for being lifted—by some enthusiasm. But Babbitt's
kind of enthusiasm, so foreign to the many, can be shared
by the few, of all races and creeds; who, whatever their
other addictions, can agree in that devotion and help to
leaven society with it.

Puzzling upon the intent of Babbitt's central doctrine,
Eliot puts the question, "What is the higher will to *will?*"
. . . and presently decides that the answer is "civilization."
But this, he claims rightly, is a very vague thing. "It is, in
fact, merely a frame to be filled with definite objects, not a
definite object itself. I do not believe that I can sit down

for three minutes to will civilization without my mind wandering to something else." That is a poignant confession; but I have a sadder one to make. I find it difficult to sit down for a short while (I shrink from the pain of estimating the exact number of minutes) to will, without wanderings of mind, any one of those virtues, at once transcendent and civilized, which I perceive that Babbitt willed with rare concentration. It is misleading to say that he willed "civilization." That is what is willed, in the modern sense of the verb "to will," by practically every modern man, woman, and child. And even if we should explain to them, as Eliot explains to us, that by "civilization" Babbitt does not mean merely "material progress, cleanliness, etc." but "a spiritual and intellectual co-ordination on a high level"—even then they would exclaim without much hesitation: "Yes, that is what we will; that's exactly our ideal, that's what we enthuse for." What Babbitt wills, however, is not mainly civilization, no matter how spiritually this may be defined. He wills, as I have suggested, certain specific virtues on which civilization ultimately depends.

But as Eliot urges that Babbitt's "higher will" is lacking in definite and objective values, it would seem that Eliot does not regard those virtues as definite and objective values. This attitude agrees entirely with the view of the many —yet Eliot is certainly one of the few. He puzzles me as much as Babbitt's higher will puzzles him. However, the fact is that, setting aside strict logic, one cannot affirm that his attitude towards the virtues is really what I have stated. It is indeed quite unclear. I must leave it to be completely investigated by the doctoral scholar for whose work this paper may serve, perhaps, as a sort of prospectus.

But, as already indicated, one point is perfectly clear. Eliot believes that a "humanistic civilization" is not feasible without church-religion; though this plain term is mine, not his. He calls attention to Babbitt's high praise of the Roman Catholic Church, even in its ultramontane aspect, as an up-holder of civilized standards. And he claims that for some of Babbitt's followers there is the danger of a "collapse into a Catholicism *without* the element of humanism and criti-cism, which would be a Catholicism of despair." One must agree. But those unhappy collapsing followers of Babbitt —just who might they be? Eliot tells us that they are "those who had followed him to the end and had found no hay in the stable." And indeed I think there would need to be an equine, even asinine, touch in the nature of such persons. But this suggestion is not intended by Eliot; he is speaking quite seriously. Therefore I must take serious objection to his metaphorical "hay." A less picturesque but clearer and fairer term would be "church-religion."

This becomes more evident near the conclusion of the essay. Here, regarding the final issue of Babbitt's philos-ophy, Eliot writes (and I shall take the liberty of inserting two numbers, obsessed as I am at present by an almost mathematical lust of clarity): 1. "It should lead, I think, to the conclusion that the humanistic point of view is auxil-iary to and dependent upon the religious point of view." 2. "For us, religion is of course Christianity; and Chris-tianity implies, I think, the conception of the Church." Now, fair and careful readers of Babbitt must know that with each of those two sentences, taken by itself, he would entirely agree; assuming that the pronoun "us" in sentence 2 means, not everyone in the world, not even everyone in Christendom, but, let's say, the large majority of occi-dental persons. I am confident that Mr. Eliot could not re-fuse to condone this exegesis of "us." However, his transi-tion from sentence 1 to sentence 2 is considerably obscurant—too obscurant in view of his declared purpose of helping to clear up "the obscurities of humanism." That transition may be termed deflective or diverting: it slides away from the fact that not all "religion" is church-religion. So that sentences 1 and 2, taken together, have the effect of identifying, for all practical purposes, "religion" and the Christian Church.

Such identification is of course rejected by Babbitt. Moreover, it is un-Christian and un-Catholic; indeed, I think it may fairly be termed heretical. For the Church, Christian and Catholic, has always maintained the doctrine implied in its Founder's declaration that He had others who are not of this fold. This doctrine is surely one of the Church's saving graces. Trodden under foot so often by the many, it has been upheld firmly by the few; and the few, in this case, have been numerous and authoritative. In short, the orthodox teaching of the Church is that there is much valid religion—that is, practical, saving religion—outside the Church.

But of course Mr. Eliot knows all this since he is an orthodox Churchman. Why, then, unlike Professor Mercier and other orthodox Churchmen, does he fail to find *any* religious validity in Babbitt's humanism? Perhaps he would reply that he *does* find it but that the point is irrelevant to the purpose of his present essay, which is concerned with the social or institutional, not with the personal or individual, mode of religion. But it is not possible to isolate those two modes from each other: I have shown that there is an unwitting slipperiness in Eliot's use of the word "religion" and the phrase "the religious point of view." Moreover, as he remarks at the beginning: "It is proverbially easier to destroy than to construct." And in his very fear (not well founded, as I have suggested, except with regard to equine

persons) that Babbittian humanism may have a destructive
effect on "religion," he runs the worse risk of destroying,
by wittily obscuring throughout this essay, the real and saving element of "religion" which that humanism has. Surely
it would have been relevant for the writer of this essay to
state plainly that, beyond terminology, Babbitt's "higher
will," even though it is unchurched, is a part of the Divine
Will which Christianity adores.

This matter is of importance for the Church; particularly,
I believe, for the Anglican Communion. Like Mr. Eliot I
am a member of that branch of the Church—unlike him, a
lifelong but sometime wandering and always very peripheral member; yet, on occasions, quite patriotic. I recall the
pleasure that I experienced on a certain day some years ago
when I learned that T. S. Eliot, so very modernistic (as he
seemed then) but so very gifted and influential a leader in
the postwar generation, had become an Anglican. But I do
not wish his view of humanism—the whole tradition of
which, not merely the Babbittian sort, is envisaged in his
essay—to be regarded as fairly representative of the Anglican outlook. He is becoming more and more a spokesman,
an able one, of the Anglo-Catholics. But his conception of
humanism is far less catholic than that of certain Roman
Catholics; notably Professor Mercier, who, unlike Mr.
Eliot, sees, and sees the value of, the traditional separation
between humane philosophy and revealed religion, while
at the same time recognizing a special religious value for
today in Babbitt's version of that philosophy.

The fact is that Eliot's essay is less valuable as a criticism
of humanism than as an expression of his own very interesting mind and, also, state of mind. He is reacting extremely, in large measure helpfully, from decadent and
popular "personal religion." He finds therein a satanically

delusive spirit, to which true religion should oppose a firm
and catholic technique. Hence his almost blasphemous epigram, "the spirit killeth, but the letter giveth life." (Elsewhere he calls attention to the fact that only the Catholic
Faith can lend real point to blasphemy.) Now, Babbitt too
criticizes that "personal religion"; but also he rejects for
himself, though he says he has no quarrel with, the principle
of external ecclesiastic authority; without which, of course,
there can be no catholic technique. In this respect, Eliot
urges, Babbitt differs extremely from the humanists of old,
who bowed to the form of religion regarded as catholic in
their day.

Certainly there is a point here, but it seems to me only
partially true and entirely superficial. Later I shall try to
outline a deeper-going critique of Babbitt which I think
Eliot touches at here but does not really grasp. He urges
that "Socrates and Erasmus were content to remain critics
and to leave the religious fabric untouched." But surely
that is essentially Babbitt's attitude also; though it is very
curious to lump those two names together over against his.
I think it would be fairer to lump Babbitt and Socrates together over against Erasmus. But Eliot remarks: "How far
Socrates believed, and whether his legendary request of the
sacrifice of a cock was merely gentlemanly behavior or even
irony, we cannot tell; but the equivalent would be Professor
Babbitt receiving extreme unction. . . ." Well, that is a very
good joke. But does Eliot mean that what he wants from
Babbitt is a kind of religious participation which *may* be
"merely gentlemanly behavior or even irony"? That, I fear,
has been the frequent attitude of the rank and file of humanists in pagan or Christian temples. But the best of them
when occasion demanded were sufficiently trenchant in
regard to popular religion, Socrates far more so, surely,

than Eliot admits, since the popular religionists determined
that an end had to be put to him. As for the Buddha, his
attitude to Hinduism seems to me even more aloof than
Babbitt's to Christianity. But speaking of Buddha and Confucius, Eliot states that by way of contrast to them "it is
always the human reason, not the revelation of the supernatural, upon which Mr. Babbitt insists." Not exactly, I
would reply. To be sure Babbitt is chary of the *word* "revelation." But what he really and mainly insists upon is an
internal revelation, that of the supernatural Will—conceived
in a trenchantly different way from that which is favored
by popular religion. Here he is close to the Buddha and in
line with Confucius.

"Confucianism," Eliot notes, "endured by fitting in with
popular religion." But most of the fitting in, I suppose, was
done by the sage's pupils and successors, not by the sage
himself. A modern parallel would be T. S. Eliot fitting in
Babbitt with popular Christianity. But instead he fits him
out, so to speak, and—unkindest cut of all—tries to un-fit
him religiously from the humanistic tradition. "His humanism is really something quite different from that of his ex-
emplars, but (to my mind) alarmingly like very liberal
Protestant theology of the nineteenth century: it is, in fact,
a product—a by-product—of Protestant theology in its last
agonies." This critical pronouncement seems to me T. S.
Eliot at his worst as a critic. It has in it just enough truth
to be specious, not enough to be true. But it is a veracious
revelation of the writer's state of mind. If to be wroth with
one we love doth work like madness in the brain, to turn
away from Babbitt's humanism, after having been its pupil,
doth certainly work one up to abnormal assertions about it.

Let the reader turn, for relieving contrast, to another and
later of Eliot's essays, that on "Catholicism and Interna-

tional Order." This to my mind is one of the most excellent of his many excellent pieces of writing. It is Catholic and catholic; it is wise, thought through, and durable. The critic's touch has here a mature and serene certainty that it lacks in the essay on Babbitt. His wit, though playing incessantly, is thoroughly subdued to the service of a grave and clear ethical purpose. He is entirely himself; yet I think that a coming investigator of the literature of our time will find here, deep down, some influence of Irving Babbitt on T. S. Eliot.

§3

The Dissension of Babbitt and More

In reading the excellent essays written upon Irving Babbitt after his death by two old friends of his, Paul E. More and W. F. Giese, I was struck by a curious point of contrast. More says of Babbitt as a graduate student at Harvard: "I can remember him stopping before a church in North Avenue and, with a gesture of bitter contempt, exclaiming, 'There is the enemy! there is the thing I hate!' Undoubtedly that sentiment was softened as time went on . . . but it never disappeared." Now, if such intense hostility to the Church was characteristic of Babbitt in his graduate days, surely it would have appeared also in his undergraduate years. For it is then, usually, that youthful hatred of the Church is most assured and declarative. But nothing of this appears in Professor Giese's careful, as well as humorous and charming, record of "Irving Babbitt, Undergraduate"; [2] though the author stresses Babbitt's inclination to supernaturalism during his four undergraduate years at Harvard.

[2] *The American Review*, November, 1935.

Quite mystified, I wrote a questioning letter to Professor Giese. He replied in part as follows: "More's quotation 'There is the enemy . . .' puzzled me quite as much as it does you. The North Avenue Church, which I. B. and I must have sauntered past a few hundred times, seemed in my day to find in him neither a friend nor a foe. His attitude appeared only aloof and indifferent. For example he was given to quoting a number of the heretical utterances of Emerson about the narrowness, the dogmatic rigidities, the inanity and ineffectiveness of the Church—the 'pulverization' of its doctrines and the ideas that would 'make the conventicles groan.' But all this seemed to me dissent rather than outright hostility. I should incline to think that the more lively hostility that More surprised in him was an expression of that profound disgust which Babbitt felt at the substitution of humanitarian preoccupations in the contemporary church for genuinely religious ones. That weakness of Protestantism Babbitt used to descant on not a little when I first knew him, just as he did later. I never felt that he at any time, early or late, exceeded these limits or condemned the Church except for its worldliness, much as he disliked its obscurantism."

That, I am sure, is a very accurate account of Babbitt's characteristic attitude towards the Church. "However," Professor Giese adds, "I drew him out very little on those matters; while More evidently discussed them to a finish in his talks with him." The phrase "to a finish" is right. Those of us who had personal relations with both More and Babbitt can testify that each of them served to accentuate the other's point of view. In their discussions they sharpened their wits upon each other; they sharpened their agreements as well as their differences. They abetted each other stoutly from first to last in forcing upon the attention of a hostile age certain deep ethical principles. But—such is the way of strenuous thinkers—the very intensity of that moral agreement heightened the intensity of their religious discord, heightened it "to a finish." This fact has to be borne in mind in reading More's memorial paper on his friend; now included, by a mournful irony of fate, in his own last volume.[3] He confided to various persons that in writing it he took extraordinary pains to·avoid saying anything that might appear at all unfair. And the essay is not only careful: it is warmly inspired. It is a rare union of acute criticism with magnanimous appreciation; it is indeed one of the most attractive of all More's writings. But, inevitably, he presents Babbitt's religious views in a categorical way which is on the whole more precise than accurate.

He contends that Babbitt believed in the supernatural but not in the superhuman, pointing out that his writings never draw a clear distinction between those two, and alleging that in Buddhism, by which he was much influenced, "the supernatural is, properly speaking, not superhuman." Probably this allegation would not be accepted by some students of Buddhism. But in any case it does not follow that Babbitt absolutely rejected the superhuman—insisted, that is, on submerging God in the supernatural "storey" of the nature of man. I know from my own conversations with Babbitt that he certainly did not do this. But I can well imagine that he would make a strong appearance of doing so in his disputations with More. In the course of his essay on his friend, More defines religion, over against Babbitt's humanism, as "an attempt to live in a plane where the supernatural departs from the natural into its own citadel of imperturbable peace." Well, I can hear, not without silent laughter, Babbitt's fulminations against such transcendental-

[3] *On Being Human*, New Shelburne Essays, Vol. III. Princeton, 1936.

ism. I can see him thrusting his jaw towards More while astringently emphasizing an "ethical will" that is not superhuman, in the sense that it does not seek to escape the world by departing "from the natural into its own citadel of imperturbable peace."

As for More's picture of Babbitt as a young college graduate giving vent to a bitter hatred of the Church, I must advance the hypothesis that this unusual outbreak was due to some provocative speech uttered by More himself but not recalled by him. For, as noted elsewhere by More, Babbitt's reactions were sometimes so overpoweringly vivid that they printed themselves on one's memory to the entire exclusion of what one had said by way of provoking them. But in any case the picturesque outburst of the youthful Babbitt against the North Avenue Church was momentary and exceptional; though naturally it seemed to More thoroughly characteristic, especially when he looked back upon it from his later standpoint of absolute Catholic dogma. Like Professor Giese and others, I found in Babbitt's talk, as in his writings, a very critical but never fundamentally hostile attitude towards the Church. He talked about it as I suppose Socrates might have talked if he had been a Harvard professor nineteen centuries after Christ, with the Protestant Reformation instead of the Homeric Age four or five hundred years behind him, and, close at hand, Emersonianism, instead of the humane mythology of the great age of Athens. In other words Babbitt maintained in modern Yankee garb the age-old bearing of the humanist, or man of critical good sense, in respect to organized religion.

But I must confess that at one time I harbored a doubt of Babbitt's consistency in this matter. Stirred by a rumor set on foot by his controversy with More, I wrote to him—as American citizens write to presidential candidates—demanding a black-and-white statement of policy on a certain point. He replied, October 4, 1929: "I agree with you that humanism should not be presented as a substitute for religion or as including religion. The notion that you seem to ascribe to me that 'organic Christianity is done with' I should regard as the height of presumption. I am much concerned with building up and fortifying the third storey of my edifice. [First storey, naturalism; second, humanism; third, religion.] I am, however, unable to assume a definitely theological position along Anglican lines; and I fear that nothing short of this would satisfy you and P.E.M., in his latest phase." The final clause of this pronouncement may be termed a countercheck courteous, penned with tongue somewhat in cheek: Babbitt knew that I did not see eye to eye with "P.E.M." For P. E. More, after cross-examining me by word of mouth and by mail as to my "theological position along Anglican lines," had pronounced me a heretic. Thus I came between the incenséd points of mighty opposites; like plenty of others who refused to take sides definitively in the religious dissension of "B & M."

"B & M"—thus some of their admirers abbreviated their names in the considerable correspondence evoked by their disputes. And that abbreviation, belonging as it does also to a well-known American railroad, struck me as a happy symbol of the mental habit of both of them. One day when Babbitt was talking to me about his friend with affectionate and extremely generous admiration, he concluded: "But as for More's theology—have you ever happened to watch him walking along the street? He marches ahead in a straight line, never looking to right or left; and that's the way he thinks." This seemed to me a pretty good description of Babbitt's thinking also; it went straight ahead like a railway. In some ways, to be sure, he was more circumspect than

More, notably in regard to theology. In this field More was trying to build tracks, forward from Plato, and back (let's say) from Princeton, to fifth-century Chalcedon, that grand central station. But both "B & M," accelerated by the impulsion of their divergence from each other, passed by at express speed a certain medial station in religion which, since the later nineteenth century, has been coming more and more to the fore.

At present its least misleading label is Liberal Catholicism. This term, to be sure, has sheltered a large variety of experimental and sometimes hopelessly heretical notions. But the main intent of the movement is the gradual building up of a modern Christian orthodoxy. That is, a religious outlook based upon the most catholic ideas and, especially, the most catholic experience and conduct discoverable in the world, no matter when or where. Discoverable supremely and awfully, however, in the words and life of Jesus Christ; and best maintained, very generally speaking, by the doctrines and practices of Christian Catholicism, which of course are not confined to those branches of the Church that wear the name of Catholic. Obviously Liberal Catholicism is an evolution from, not a revolution against, traditional Catholicism. But Catholicism ceases to be catholic in so far as it clings to concepts that are at variance with the continual revelation of truth in life. The Liberal Catholic holds the conviction that truth, like life, is never miraculous in the sense of "unnatural" or "lawbreaking." He holds this conviction, not because it is modern, but because it is catholic. He rejects as uncatholic the modern notion that the deepest laws of life are comprehensible (not just apprehensible) by the human mind, are clearer now than ever before, and are to be opposed to the Christian revelation. He rejects so-called "Modernism" in religion, whether Protestant or Catholic. But he knows that the doctrines and practices of the Church must be modernly revised.

That summary of the Liberal Catholic position, which I suppose has had its fullest scope so far in the Anglican Communion, is certainly very inadequate. But it will serve for my present purpose, which is to point out that this position was not taken into account, properly and critically, by our two leading American critics, Babbitt and More. They passed it by on the other side—on opposite sides from each other. More, however, in the upshot, gave it a wider berth than Babbitt. Such at least is my opinion, paradoxical as it may seem to some, and as it would certainly seem to Babbitt and More themselves. My own experience of them in this matter is typical enough to be recounted without apology; incidentally it is not unamusing.

Each of them said to me, separately, these identic words: "I cannot see how you can call yourself an Anglican." But Babbitt meant, "Aren't you embarrassed?" More meant, "I am sure you are wrong." He said, in effect: "You and others like you are really breaking away from the Anglican and Catholic form of the Christian faith, but you refuse to face this fact, thus deceiving yourselves and others." Now, More's own religious views were in many ways liberal and in a few points, I believe, decidedly heretical (this sounds, of course, like tit for tat). But in certain respects which seemed to him fundamental his standpoint was opposed uncompromisingly to that, I should say, of Liberal Catholicism, though he himself would not put the matter that way. He believed that his standpoint was as liberal as was possible without ceasing to be Catholic.

But it is with Babbitt's case that I am here mainly concerned. He said to me in effect: "Of course, these matters are outside my province, but I find it hard to understand

how anyone holding your very modern views can go in for
the creeds and exercises of the Episcopal Church." I tried
hard on various occasions to unravel this mystery for him,
but he kept me explaining my explanations and the process
had no end. At times I fancied that he was grasping my
point of view, but soon some or other remark would make
me see that (in a phrase from Frost's poetry) his mind had
let go of it. Once he informed me that the species of Christianity with which he had been "surrounded" during his
boyhood in the Middle West had alienated him from ecclesiastic forms of worship. "But apparently," he added,
comically trying to subdue the irony in his voice and eyes,
"your luck has been much better."

By temperament and circumstance, though not at all "in
principle" (as the diplomats say), he was averse to the
Anglican Communion. And I found that he had practically
no acquaintance with the considerable literature of Liberal
Catholicism. Otherwise he might have discovered that this
movement had much in common with his own humanism,
particularly with his doctrines of the religious imagination
and the higher will. Also he would have found that the
direction of that movement was away from the kind of
Christology which More had come to consider essential
but which he himself was far from able to accept. In spirit,
More was further from the Liberal Catholic outlook, and
Babbitt closer to it, than either of them realized.

So far as I could discover, the only modern theological
books with which Babbitt was really familiar were those of
More! This situation seemed to me at once natural and odd,
amusing and pathetic. Natural enough was his lack of familiarity with theology in general. It was outside his "field
of concentration," as the phrase runs in our American universities; and owing to Harvard—and Babbitt—his leisure

was abnormally slight. But it was also natural that he should make an exception in favor of the work of More, his old friend and new theological enemy. However, it was very unfortunate that he should miss the significance of such religious writers as Von Hügel and A. E. Taylor—his contemporaries and, I think, his natural allies—while studying the later books of More with an extreme though antagonistic deference. In conversation he would praise with bated breath More's ability as writer and thinker—then sharply attack his latest point of view. "But as for you Episcopalians," he would say to me with grave reproach, "you ought to regard More as a new tower of strength to your cause." He could not forgive the failure of the Anglican Communion to welcome with great éclat the accession of More to the fold. And he was inclined to deem that failure typical— one more instance of a certain dubiety in the Anglican position, of a certain lack of grip and force in the Anglican mentality. He could not see how the new Anglican, More, could be less important than the lifelong Roman Catholic, Von Hügel, for current Anglican thought, or, more widely speaking, for Liberal Catholicism.

From such enigmas his mind would turn with relief to the spectacle of the Roman Catholic Church with its clearcut dogmas and wide social efficiency. He contrasted it, to its great advantage, with the Orthodox Church of the East, which had made such a dreadful mess of things in Russia. As for the great Christian federation that might in time ensue from the growing *rapprochement* of the Anglican and Orthodox communions—well, we must hope for the best. Babbitt did not (T. S. Eliot to the contrary) place all the hopes of humanity on one institution, the Roman Catholic Church. I recall his swift rebuke of a person who asserted in his presence that the Protestant churches were doomed. Such a pronunciamento, he said, was highly presumptuous; such an attitude of mind was far from humanistic. His point was simply that, so far, the Roman Church had shown more capacity than other religious bodies to face social reality and to uphold civilized standards. However, it is undeniable that his admiration for that church as a working institution helped to confirm his opinion that Christian doctrine, to be workable, had to be old-fashioned.

This opinion appears in certain passages of his posthumous volume, *The Dhammapada, Translated from the Pāli with an Essay on Buddha and the Occident.*⁴ But before dealing with those passages I must remark upon the very special value of this book as a whole. For those who read between the lines it reveals more intimately than Babbitt's previous works the things by which he daily lived. His translation of the ancient poem—the Buddha's Sermon on the Mount, as it has been called—throws its English predecessors into the shade. They suffer heavily from romantic coloration. His version, though sometimes awkward, has a powerful simplicity that takes hold of the reader and does not let him go. The prose in which the old verses are rendered is a fine kind of modern poetic prose; though that statement would doubtless surprise Babbitt himself. Aiming only at truth, he here attains poetry also. The spectacle of Babbitt in this role is striking and refreshing; but only on the surface is it strange and surprising. Babbitt the man had a richer love of poetry than Babbitt the critic could show. And this beautiful translation is the natural result of his close familiarity with the Buddhist scriptures; it is the ripe fruit of long love and deep conviction.

The poem prepares the reader happily for the ensuing essay on "Buddha and the Occident." The essay is a final

⁴ London, 1936.

fusion of the many thoughts on this subject that run through Babbitt's works. It is packed, sometimes repetitious and clumsy, but on the whole profound and indispensable. It shows the great service that Buddhist ideas can render to thoughtful persons in the West at the present crisis of our civilization. More engagingly, it reveals, between the lines, when studied in close connection with his rendering of the Dhammapada, how much the Buddha meant to the author himself.

As for the religious bearing of the essay, some readers will decide—sadly if they are Christians, gladly if they are anti-Christians—that the author's deep-laid design is to promote Buddhism at the expense of Christianity. That sort of reader cannot be helped. It is clear enough to an unprejudiced reader that the writer's main intention, as indicated by his closing sentence, is to bring out what those two religions have deeply in common. Also he wishes to show how the Buddha's way of thought may act as a corrective for popular Christianity. No doubt this secondary aim is developed disproportionally; but naturally, in view of the fact that the author is first and last a critic; and helpfully, in view of the present problems of Christendom. These considerations ought to be borne in mind while contemplating the three passages which I am going to quote below. For the sake of fairness they ought to be read in their context.[5] But my present purpose requires me to extract them and to append in each case some critical remarks.

1. "It is hard to see how one can affirm, on strictly experimental grounds, a personal God and personal immortality. If a man feels that these tremendous affirmations are necessary for his spiritual comfort, he should turn to dogmatic and revealed religion which alone can give them."

5 See p. 80.

Of course, the words "personal" and "comfort" have each a higher and a lower sense which are not considered by the writer. But my main point is that the words "experimental" and "revealed" are thrown into a false, obsolescent opposition. *Experimental revelation,* so to call it, is the ground of the two "tremendous affirmations" mentioned by the writer. They would better be termed "dim but vital instincts." Certainly they are not *given,* as Babbitt puts it, by dogmatic religion. This merely formulates them.

2. "What one is able to affirm without going beyond immediate experience and falling into dogma is, in Arnold's phrase, a great power not ourselves that makes for righteousness, a phrase that reminds one of Buddha's conception of the *dhamma,* or human law, as one may render it, in contradiction to the law of physical nature." Certainly "immediate experience," when it is authoritative, affirms that moral "power" or "dhamma." But to claim as Babbitt does that immediate experience cannot also affirm divine personality, that this belongs only to the sphere of dogma, is to weaken the authority of immediate experience; thus weakening, implicitly, its affirmation of moral law. Immediate experience, when it is entire, affirms a Being that is at once Personality and Law, in the highest sense of these two words.

3. "Not being able to find any personality human or divine superior to his own, Buddha got his humility, as he himself tells us, by looking up to the Law." No irony, unfortunately, is intended here. The writer unwittingly makes us feel the limitation of the Buddhistic kind of humility. Certainly it is great and true so far as it goes; this is what one feels in reading the *Dhammapada,* particularly the present version. But the Buddha's humility is really an abstraction from entire religious humility; just as his supernatural Law is an abstraction from the complete Supernature,

wherein Law has life more abundantly. Only when the divine life is experienced as in the highest sense personal, can human persons look up to it with entire humility.

In short, those three passages are very far from Babbitt's best. They seem to me so outstandingly naïve and weak in comparison with the rest of the essay that I must believe they are due to the heat of his contention with More. Heat checks light when close friends differ. The increasing warmth of More's criticism of Buddhistic thought led Babbitt to make uncircumspect assertions on behalf of it. And, as previously noted, Babbitt believed that the Christian Gospel according to Paul E. More was far more canonical than it really is. In the first and second passages above, the sharp (yet obtuse) opposition between "dogmatic and revealed religion" on the one hand, and, on the other, "experimental" or "immediate" experience, is quite in line with More's theological thought. But while More harshly subordinated experience to ancient Christian dogma, Babbitt strove to fortify experience by delimiting and hardening its bounds over against dogma. His stand in this matter was far more occasional than More's; not essential to his main position; comparatively tentative. Hence he begins in the first passage with the saving, or somewhat saving, clause, "It is hard to see." Paul E. More, I think, would have written "It is impossible to see." Otherwise, however, that first sentence might just as well have been penned by More as by Babbitt. Its thought, misleading and antiquated, was one which the two friends, arguing face to face on opposite sides of the fence, helped each other to maintain. In short, a considerable price had to be paid, religiously, for their moral co-operation.

§4

THE RELIGIOUS IMAGINATION

The critical co-operation of Babbitt and More for almost half a century on behalf of "humanism" will be seen in the future as an important episode, unique after its fashion, in the story of human culture. Together they bore the heat and dust of a crucial battle of ideas, crucial especially in America. Each contributed what the other lacked: More, distinguished literary art and scope; Babbitt, personal force and spiritual dedication. Their conjunction was providential; but, like all gifts of providence, it had to be paid for. As I have tried to show, their intimacy accentuated their constitutional differences in religious outlook. Their debate, in the end, seemed to open a chasm between humanism and religion. In reality the chasm was a superficial fissure. Beneath it there was a certain deep agreement: the two men had in common a humane, catholic conception of the religious imagination. That conception was concealed by their growing divergence in religious concepts; the concepts dimmed the conception. Also, their temperamental limits prevented them from developing that conception so as to bring it fully to bear on modern religious needs. I wish now to deal with this situation as it appears in the case of Babbitt.

I recall his exclaiming, characteristically, when talking of the various schools of current criticism: "The imagination —that's what we're all fighting for!" His continual stress upon the decisive power of the imagination in all human affairs was piquant, even poignant, in the case of a person who had not very much imagination himself. No doubt he would have more or less despised it if he had lived in the middle of the eighteenth century. And if, thereto, he had been an orthodox member of the Church of England he would probably have found nothing to smile at in Doctor Johnson's famous remark to the effect that, since Christianity was so beneficent a system for mankind, God had quite properly set aside the laws of nature in order to establish it. Johnson was religious, but deficient in imaginational flexibility. The same is true of Babbitt; but his critical outlook, unlike Johnson's, comprised, ór at least involved, the full significance of imagination. For he was keenly aware of neoclassic criticism's failure in this respect, and of the disastrous results (so he called them) that ensued by way of reaction when Romanticism seized the helm. More importantly, his study of Greek and oriental literature, including the Bible, made him fully conscious of the fact that the highest kind of truth comes to man only through the imagination.

But in his treatment of this matter there is a certain paradox. I can best bring out what I mean by presenting a review of his sixth book, the last to be published before his death, *On Being Creative and Other Essays* (1932). This, I think, is his most "popular" work, if that adjective may be applied to any of his writings. A new reader of Babbitt might be advised to begin with it (if not with his posthumous volume, considered above) because of its obvious timeliness. But this very quality brought upon it exceptional mistreatment on the part of popular reviewers: the author trod heavily upon notions beloved by them, and they, in return, tried to tread upon him. Letters of protest written by Babbitt's admirers to the journals in question were not printed. In fact, it was very rarely that even able, temperate, and interesting letters (I have seen some of them in manuscript) written on behalf of any book by Babbitt or More were accepted by periodical editors. Journals loudly in favor of a frank and free expression of all ideas made an exception in *dis*favor of the ideas of Babbitt and More.[6] I suppose that the editors wished to show by rank unfairness that they considered the humanistic way of thought rankly unfair. May they rest in peace! . . . I tried hard to be fair to Babbitt's ideas, for and against, in my review of *On Being Creative* in the *Saturday Review of Literature*, June 4, 1932, and I am going to try still harder in the ensuing revision and expansion of that article.

This book is timely, powerful, and interesting. A deep vein of meditation goes through it, and its pages are alive with swift and witty reflections, ranging all the way from Confucius and the old East to Theodore Dreiser and the new West. The central chapter, on "Coleridge and the Imagination," takes its place unmistakably among the few best critical essays in our language. The main theme of the volume is the present state of imagination in literature, morals, and religion. The author believes that this most potent of all human faculties is today very degenerate. It is badly decomposed. He calls for a reinvigoration, a reintegration, of the imagination. His thesis may be summarized as follows.

During the past two centuries the imagination has become associated more and more with sheer spontaneity; and today this quality has reached its nadir. Our imaginative writers are pursuing spontaneity and originality to the point of achieving, as Babbitt puts it, "the ultimate worm's-eye view of life." They are wriggling "from depth to depth

---

[6] I recall that when a notoriously brutal and bad-tempered review of a book by More appeared in one of our most liberal journals, my letter of protest to the editor was returned with a little, unintentionally comic note, saying, "I think your communication is not good-tempered enough."

of triviality." Any experience that any individual may have
at any time, so long as it appears to be spontaneous, is assumed to have the right to sway his imagination. Hence our
young people are growing up in an atmosphere of "self-
expression" that befogs the vital meaning (not just the
moral meaning) of moral principles, since these, though
vitally important for true self-development, do not belong
to "self-expression" in the current degenerate sense of this
term. As for our advanced religionists, they, in their anxiety
to be free from old dogmas, are freeing themselves from
the ancient "facts of human nature"—in favor of "creative
emotion." We have fallen into "a veritable cant on the subject of creation." This word, in defiance of its root meaning, has now become synonymous with spontaneous com-
bustion, with sheer temperamental effervescence.

Originality having come to such a pass, Babbitt suggests
that "the most original thing one could do nowadays would
be to question the whole theory of originality as mere temperamental overflow that has prevailed since the eighteenth
century." A critically detached view of that theory could
lead us to revive, in fresh form, the ancient idea of *imitation.* This idea at its best does not mean bondage: it means
true human freedom. Our individual lives are so little, so
"rounded with a sleep," that spontaneity is slavery when it
submerges us in the flux of our passing experiences. To win
freedom we must focus our imagination upon "the true
human universal"; that is, upon what is found to be central
in human experience as a whole. This does not mean the
abrogation of vital individuality. For the human universal
is not an absolute category, a rigid fixture. It is "a oneness
that is always changing." But it provides us with workable
standards. And only in bringing these standards to bear
upon our individual lives may we achieve real personality

instead of mere particularism; rich and shapely spontaneity instead of sheer effusion; and true creativeness instead of "a subrational parody" of it. Right imitation—the effort to guide and shape our own experiences in the light of the universal—is truly creative.

Babbitt urges that creative imitation is fundamentally an effort of the will, and that what we mainly suffer from today is "a subtle psychic indolence." We are averse to the "spiritual strenuousness" required for a rediscovery and re-application of the human universal. We are apt to resent the very idea of a universal will, or self, if it is conceived as "an inner principle of control set above our temperamental selves" and demanding from us a certain self-limitation, concentration, and even renunciation. We protect ourselves against that idea by regarding it as outworn and negative, instead of life-giving and life-renewing. Hence modern man has tended to lose entirely the belief that "there is an immortal essence presiding like a king over his appetites" (quoted from Walter Lippmann by Babbitt with high approval).

Therefore the great question is, how may our faith in that "immortal essence" be revived? How may our will to follow its behests be reinvigorated? In two ways, according to the author: 1. Through "dogmatic and revealed religion" —which, however, has become impossible for many modern persons including the author himself; 2. Through a reassertion of "the higher will" on purely experiential grounds, apart from theism and all other theological dogmas. This way requires a fresh and critical restudy of the great saints and sages of all dispensations. Their common moral or spiritual essence must be extracted, so to speak, from its dogmatic embodiments and reaffirmed in modern psychologic

form. Now, Babbitt makes clear that he has no quarrel with
Way 1. He sees that it can mean, though too often it does
not mean, a reinforcement of moral principles by the religious imagination. But apparently he does not perceive that
Way 2, by itself, may have a depressing and even disruptive
effect upon the imagination, which, surely, cannot live by
vitamines alone. How can there be an *imaginational* communion (as well as a moral communion) between the devotees of Way 1 and the devotees of Way 2? Yet this book
calls for a thorough reintegration of imagination. Such is the
paradox.

The present sick state of the imagination would seem to
require primarily the revival of great images, or types of
image, which in the past have represented that which is
central and universal in human experience. For instance,
the god-man and the altar. The story of these twin symbols,
coming down through many religions in many lands and
culminating in Christianity, is the story of man's effort to
grasp, through imagination, that very truth of the High
Will and vital self-sacrifice which Babbitt advocates. Of
course he himself is well aware of this fact. But he relin-
quishes those symbols to the keeping of a static kind of
Christianity (including certain outstanding features of the
Christological thought of Paul E. More), which, as he says,
has become impossible for many modern persons. He does
so in face of the historic fact that those symbols are very
far from static. Essentially they remain the same, but they
are open always to mental reinterpretation. Indeed they are
part—to use Babbitt's own fine phrase—of "a oneness that is
always changing." They have always been and will always
be subject to revision in crucial times; and, as Babbitt knows
so well, ours is such a time. To work for a "re-vision" of

those symbols in the light of the ideas provided by Way 2 is to work for an imaginational integration of Way 1 and Way 2.

No doubt this line of thought lays one open to suspicion on the part of very orthodox and of very unorthodox persons. They, from their opposite standpoints, are quick to bring the charge of poetic self-deception against those of my persuasion. They feel that we are trying to substitute poetry for religion. They accuse us of sentimental Catholicism. They may consign us to the fold of George Santayana; who, according to a well-known witticism, believes (or used to believe) that "there is no God and that Mary is His Mother." However, those who hold the view which I am following believe that there certainly is a God and that, in a very real sense, the Blessed Mary is his mother. We catch, or wish to catch, the full force of a passage in the writings of the late G. K. Chesterton concerning the truth and splendor "of the idea of the Mother of God." Later in this book I shall touch more fully upon the subject of Christology. Here I may remark that more than once in the past the style of Santayana, in respect to the Christian religion, has reminded me of the great moving serpent in the ninth book of Milton's *Paradise Lost:* intricately beautiful in its "circling spires," burnished, superb—and fatal.

Certainly we must beware of the religion of poetry; but the surest safeguard against it, in the long run, is the poetry of religion. Of course the two are often closely intertwined. Milton's charming snake, according to the tale that he told to Eve (a fictitious but meaningful tale), could wind himself about the trunk of the Tree of the Knowledge of Good and Evil and eat his fill of fruit too high for all other beasts. Clearly, however, he could not reach the outmost and lof-

tiest sprays where, I fancy, the fruit attained its fullest
maturity. It was protected from him by the natural and
complete—the poetic—growth of the Tree. . . . Or we may
say that the religion of poetry is a parasitic vine supported
by the tree of religion. If the tree is of vigorous growth
with overtopping foliage it cannot be smothered by the
vine. This is the natural and, in the end, the only certain
defense of the tree. No doubt there are times when it needs
to have its parasite severely pruned. But in such case there
is the danger that the branches of the tree will be injured,
or even severed, along with the intertwining limbs of the
vine. This danger attended the critical methods of Babbitt
and More. To be sure, there was an abnormal need.

The decline of religious catholicity in the Occident before, during, and after the Protestant Reformation meant
an extraordinary damage to the poetry of religion. The
germ of that situation was planted long before, namely
when the Roman Empire joined hands with the Christian
Church. The immense advantage to the Church of the
Roman genius for organization has been heavily paid for
by what Christianity has suffered from the Roman defect
in poetry. Scholars have shown ever more clearly that the
chief imaginational developments of Christianity originated
in the provinces, not in the Roman mind. Rome could accept, adapt, or carry on poetry but was deficient in poetic
origination and in poetic, as distinguished from strategic,
flexibility. No wonder that Christendom has had increasingly to draw upon the religious imagination of the Greeks
and the Orientals. Romanistic legalism in theology and in
polity was furiously accentuated throughout the Christian
Church, Catholic and Protestant, by the dissensions of the
Reformation. (How the question as to whether the Protestants or the Catholics are the more to blame can best be

answered, God knows.) The result was a shrinkage and hardening of the poetry of Christianity; a phenomenon not new, but of a scope and grievousness quite unprecedented, in the history of religion. People turned from Christianity to seek their daily bread of poetry elsewhere.

Hence there rose a huge growth of poetic substitutes for religion; that is, for true religion. The substitutes nourished themselves, religiously and surreptitiously, on the Christian spirit. The parasitic foliage was like to stifle the tree. This possibility has loomed very large in America, particularly, and the sharp blade of criticism wielded by More and Babbitt against specious spirituality was certainly called for. Their significance is very far from being merely cisatlantic; but their extraordinary trenchancy, with its virtues and limitations, resulted from the acuteness of the American situation. Posit an Emerson in the expansive America of the earlier nineteenth century, a Babbitt and More will follow two generations later. Certainly the religion of poetry was not the center of Emerson; it was just his atmosphere. But he with his greatness gave great countenance to it; and our two critics determined to give it none at all. They set their faces so severely against the religion of poetry in all its modern forms that they were not in position to assist in developing the modern form of the poetry of religion.

Babbitt could not see that great religious images can be reaffirmed, no less than "the higher will," on "purely experiential grounds," assuming, as he assumed, that these grounds comprise the best experience of the past as well as of the present. We may, if we wish, reject or depreciate the religious imagination. But if we accept it in its full significance, as Babbitt wished to do, then we ought to see that it demands today a revitalization of perennial religious symbols. Our faith must be that these are not *merely* symbols, that their essence is reality; and that if they undergo a process of criticism which is at once sympathetic and open-eyed, and esthetic as well as moral, they will be found in accord with whatever is valid in modern thought and experience.

That process, of course, is a large order. But I am sure that it is a way ahead for criticism at the present time, particularly in America. It is a proper sequel to the work of Babbitt and More. It moves towards that reintegration of imagination which they saw to be so necessary and for which they built strong moral and intellectual bases. But it is a *via media* closer to the truth of imagination than the two disjunct ways envisaged by Babbitt and, with a different emphasis, by More also. It is the way of healing the discord—more apparent than real in the case of those two critics, but deadly in so far as real—between religion and humanism.

PART TWO

6.

Life Dramatic

§1

O NE CLOUDLESS DAY AT THE HEIGHT OF SUMMER, TWO large deep-sea fish swam higher than they had ever swum before. I shall not attempt to explain their behavior in terms of the facts of submarine life as viewed by Dr. William Beebe and other deep-going scientists, my aim here being theological rather than ichthyological. The time was noon; the water without a ripple; and the downpour of sunshine amazingly strong. It penetrated the ocean to the depth of many feet—or tails: it gleamed on the scales of my two fish. They waved their fins and goggled with unusual animation. The elder, whose Christian name was Moses, asserted solemnly: "This dim illumination comes down from our Creator, the Great Round Sun-Fish, ninety million whales'-lengths away. He dwells in a vast invisible liquid above the surface of our little ocean. But He can come down and ——"

"You poor superstitious fish," the other gurgled sibilantly; then he performed a long-headed, elliptical smile. Julian, as he was called, proceeded: "My friend, you love to loll in the sluggish currents of outworn traditions. Why not face the plain *fax?*" (The full articulation of "facts" is very hard for fish.) "The truth is, there is nothing at all above the so-called surface of the sea. Indeed there is no such surface, except in the dreams of superficial fishes. Why credit the airy fancies of the self-inflated little creatures known as flying fish? As for this warm, green luminescence

about us, certainly it must *seem* to you to come down from
above so long as you insist on rolling your eyes upwards in
that pietistic, quite unpiscine fashion. But really, it comes
from below. See straight and you will see that it rises from
the depths beneath us. It is a phosphorescent shimmer
thrown up by that dark, vast, fathomless Reality from
which we fish are evolved."

"But how do you know it is fathomless?" Moses inquired.
"And what is it that does the evolving? And how can light
come out of darkness that is all dark? I, too, wish to face
the fax; but I wish to face them all."

Julian gave him a white-edged glance of scorn. "You
don't know fax from bubbles," he began—then suddenly
darted away after his dinner, which happened to be passing.
Moses watched the swirlings fade, brooding gillfully. Then
he glided upwards, very, very slowly, through increasing
radiance—until his sensations warned him to desist. He
knew that his constitution differed decidedly from that of
flying fishes. He had no desire to explode! Also, it was dinnertime. He looked down around.

§2

When we try to face all the facts, we see that human life
is always a kind of drama, whatever else it is or may be. Of
course it has been given innumerable other names: a dream,
a stream, a game, a trial, a mechanism, a growth, a final result, a preparation. . . . And no doubt every name is true in
its way; it represents what some people have sometimes
found in life. One finding is "a stream." But of course there
are streams and streams. If I should declare that the stream
called "Suez Canal" is an excellent image of human life, the
reader, I trust, would disagree. His thoughts would fly to a

river, some river that he loves, one with a richly varied course; and his mind would dwell less on its smooth canal-like reaches than on those where the current copes with twisting banks and rocks and falls. That is, if the reader is one who has had considerable experience of life; not if he has always lived, untroubled, on the income of his income. The point being that life is dramatic, that a river is more dramatic than a canal, and that some reaches of a river are much more dramatic than others. Normally (I would claim) we find every image of life to be more or less appealing as it is more or less dramatic.

For me and, I think, for many others—though not for such as the poet Shelley—a stream is more interesting when it has a fisherman on it or in it; on it in a boat, or in it with boots up to his groins. Not that I myself am fond of fishing (except for images) but it is a kind of game, and games are on the whole more dramatic than streams. Persons who are sufficiently alive prefer "the game of life" to "the stream of life." But of course there are games and games. Fishing is one of the least dramatic. Still less so is solitaire. An elderly placid spinster, who spends much of her time at it, may regard life as mainly a game of solitaire. But football, surely, is a far more adequate emblem; and then there are the greater games of commerce and love and politics and war.

"Life is a battle." Think of all the drama in that old saying; then place alongside it, "Life is a mechanism." Certain thinkers in ancient times and, again, during the past two centuries managed to conceive the universe, including human life, as a self-running machine, thus pretty well blotting all "the battle" out of the picture—to the eye of common sense, at least. For common sense knows that life cannot be really battalious if it is in the main a self-running machine. But common sense also knows that life has in it a large mechanical element. At times we exclaim, or feel like exclaiming, "Life is just one damn thing after another!" It appears to us, in such moods, not only a self-running but a useless and unaccountable machine. Those moods, when we emerge from them, are recognized as abnormal. Yet they point to a reality, to the immense amount of machinery that there is in our universe. But of course, so far as human experience goes—and in this essay I wish to go no further—machinery can never run itself, in the long run. The machine for perpetual motion will probably need to be attended to every billion years or so. In any case it will need to be attended to at the first: it will need to be invented. And it will be known perpetually in *Who's Who* as the invention of Somebody. A machine is a personal contrivance. The so-called "mechanical genius" of a great inventor is very personal indeed, as all real genius is. A machine is contrived by that part of Somebody which is not a machine.

To contrive is human. Battle, especially, is full of devices. In the main, however, war is not contrivance but inspiration. As fighting is very costly, men contrive not to fight until they are inspired, for good or ill, to do so. Then their inspiration seizes upon and subordinates, transforms and quickens, all their powers of contrivance. Strictly speaking, all contrivance goes back to inspiration. When we say of some design that it is "utterly uninspired" we mean that its inspiration is very slight or secondhand. Nor can inspiration be real without contrivance. So-called inspiration that cannot at all contrive to assume intelligible form would better be called "spiration." Inspiration is really the ultimate spirit of contrivance. In actuality the two are continually opposed, because life is a battle. But they are not intrinsically hostile to each other, because life is less a battle than it is a drama. The struggle of inspiration with contrivance is dramatic. Not "*merely* dramatic," as we say of a cloud battle in a storm; that is, comparatively unreal. It is all the more real because it is highly and thoroughly dramatic. It is vital and fruitful. Contrivance, like Jacob in his struggle with his angel, wins by losing. Contrivance must put forth all its strength, testing the quality of its friendly opponent; but in the upshot, contrivance gains when inspiration wins. Wherever life is, there is contrivance. But life is most dramatic when a superb, complex contrivance—for example, the personality of a St. Paul—is mastered, transformed and fulfilled by a sublime inspiration.

§3

The stage drama is the most contriving, the most artful, of all the arts. Hence it is generally the tawdriest. But hence, too, it can be uniquely comprehensive: it can draw a multitude of other arts into its service. And because it is so rich in contrivance it can be the milieu of opulent inspiration. Shakespeare inherited a large array of dramatic devices and conventions which he was able to inspire with fresh vitality. His work, so our schoolbooks say, is surpassingly true to life. More exactly, it is true to a certain sphere and phase of life; namely, the civic life of man in its modern, thoroughly mundane form.

Certainly this phase of life is very dramatic in its way. That it is also dramatic in the fullest and most real sense of the term, has been a growing belief since the sixteenth century. But nowadays many are aware that our modern preoccupation with the drama of mundane civic life—immensely quickened during the past hundred years by the phenomenal advance of practical science and industry—is abnormal, "untrue to nature." It has led to disillusion, to the feeling that the world is just a stage and "all the men and women *merely* players." Such a result was prophesied in many verses of our modern bible, the Works of Shakespeare; especially in the later plays, written while the King James Bible was in course of preparation—a profound coincidence, the simultaneity of those two authorized but different versions of life. The Shakespearean drama is a great city with stately mansions, busy streets, and laughing rustic suburbs. But it has no sacred hills around and no temple at its center. The citizens, so "true to nature," as we say, are remarkably cut off from Universal Nature. No doubt that was the necessary condition of the author's extraordinary success. His city is a "close-up" of a fascinating mien of life. He could know, and show, his people with such intense nearness only by assembling them in an isolated foreground, away from the epic gods and mountains that had hitherto dominated literature and drama, Christian and pre-Christian. But a heavy price had to be paid for that splendid isolation. The more completely we have been entranced by the great city, Shakespeare's and ours, the more we feel in the end the force of his great lyric cry when his work (together with the King James Bible) was just about finished: "This insubstantial pageant . . . our little life."

But such was certainly *not* the judgment of Shakespeare the man upon life as a whole. The late G. K. Chesterton remarked that every Catholic reader knows that Shakespeare was a Catholic; and, in a broad sense, this, I am sure, is true. Shakespeare, albeit very much a man of the world, had a catholic Christian standpoint. He viewed the universe as a creation wherein personality and love are supreme creative powers. Early passages in his plays, such as Portia's speech on mercy and King Henry the Fourth's crusading proem (celebrating "those holy fields over whose acres

walked those blessed feet") prepare for the greater utterance in *Measure for Measure*, when he was approaching
the height of his tragic period:

> Alas! Alas!
> Why, all the souls that were were forfeit once;
> And He that might the vantage best have took,
> Found out the remedy. How would you be
> If He, which is the top of judgment, should
> But judge you as you are? O! think on that,
> And mercy then will breathe within your lips,
> Like man new made.

Such a passage is recognized as close to the heart of its author; not mainly because of its rare force and conviction,
which might be attributed to the speaker, the would-be
nun, Isabella; but because it represents the attitude of
Shakespeare in his total writings. Love, he always knows,
is "the top of judgment." He treats his characters with high
Christian charity and with a deep sense of the divine-human
mystery of redemption. But just because of his catholic
Christian outlook, Shakespeare knows that life *under the
aspect of a merely mundane drama* is indeed "the baseless
fabric of a vision." His special capability as an artist was
for civic plot and dialogue. But his catholicity of spirit as
a man made him feel keenly the comparative unreality of
the quick words and structures of modern civic life.

He did not profoundly believe in the mundane civic
drama but in Life itself. Hence the not infrequent lightness
of his artistic conscience, his nonchalant violations of dramatic probability. And hence (i.e., because of his faith in
Life) the modest cheerfulness which characterized him as a
man among men, according to the records, and which is

certainly the dominant tone of his work as a whole. No doubt he had moods of deep-going pessimism. But he would be shocked, I am sure, by the fundamental disbelief in life which many modern Hamlets have read into his plays. It is hard to say whether he would be more shocked than amused by the scriptural solemnity of many of his modern adorers—by the spectacle of his works placed on a level with the Bible, or above that level, as a fundamental interpretation of human life; by hearing himself termed "the sole universal genius," etc. In fact, he is universally urbane, not universally universal. He is lacking in a faculty which he himself, I believe, would rank above his own abilities and which is certainly universal in the truest sense—the mythological imagination.[1]

That faculty is man's sovereign means of interpreting the universe and of realizing, practically, his own place therein. Therefore it is the supreme faculty in the realm of art. Which of course does not necessarily mean that the leading mythological poets were greater artists than Shakespeare. The comparative merits of him and Dante, for instance, may better be settled when our perspective is better, say one or two thousand years hence. But assume, in accordance with the present prevailing opinion, that Shakespeare is quite peerless, so far. This would merely mean that human art has reached its highest level, so far, in the sphere of the mundane civic drama. A still higher level may be attained some day in a greater sphere, one that will not exclude the mythologic imagination.

This gift of the gods to man is so great that it requires for its development the whole of human history, which, ac-

---

[1] The assimilation of "myth" to "legend" is characteristic of the modern age. Properly, a myth is the story of an action in which the divine and the human mingle. The lowest myth must have some truth; the highest must be supremely true in its meaning.

cording to new science as well as old instinct, lies mainly
ahead of us. The mythologic imagination, just because it is
supreme in the realm of art, is slow in becoming supremely
artistic. Ancient innumerable efforts preceded the perfection of Greek epic and drama. From the standpoint of
Greek art at its best, the rest of the vast realm of pagan
mythopoesy is a crude chaos. But from the standpoint of
Christianity at its best, Greek mythopoesy itself is a very
primitive shapeliness. And Christianity—still comparatively
new in the world—may in the future produce works of art
greater than those inspired by its medieval phase, i.e., from
the thirteenth to the seventeenth century. Supreme Christian drama (not to speak of Christian epic) remains to be
created. The inchoate religious drama of the later Middle
Ages, unlike that of the early Greeks, was estopped in its
development by the rise of secularism. Shakespeare came,
instead of a Christian Sophocles. Yet Shakespeare's *dramatis
personae* owe their unique "reality" to the value which the
Christian Faith revealed, uniquely, in human persons. Our
modern secular drama is largely the result of Christianity;
and it may be reabsorbed into the Christian outlook. Indeed, unless this is to occur, it is hard to see any great future for the drama, since it has now exhausted its chief secular motives.[2]

Some great dramatic poet of the future, combining the
arts of Sophocles and Shakespeare, may create, for the stage,
persons who are "real," as we say—that is, psychologically
complex and vivid—but whose story will have for its background the sublime Christian mythology. They will be

[2] Just as I am revising this essay, certain journals are announcing the
remarkable success on the stage of T. S. Eliot's drama on Becket, *Murder
in the Cathedral*. I gather that it is emphatic in its Christian standpoint,
unlike Tennyson's fine Victorian play, completed in 1879, on the same
subject; and I hope it shows the way the dramatic wind is blowing.

overseen and visited by gods and demigods. Mythic "machinery," as we call it scornfully because it is dead to us,
or we are dead to it, will become alive and organic again.
So will the inward struggles of the persons of the drama.
Shakespeare and all good dramatists, including several who
have written plays concerned with the World War, know
that man's inner conflicts are more truly dramatic than his
outward battlings. Indeed the human moral struggle is the
very heart and center of the drama. But during the eighteenth century it came to seem unreal, a merely civic phenomenon, unrelated to the heart and center of the universe.
Therefore the drama literally lost heart: its pulse was extremely faint a hundred years ago. But recently it has been
taking or trying to take heart again, groping for its true
center. And in the Christian mythopoetic drama of the future, the human moral struggle will appear again as a divine
conflict—derived from and belonging to the heart of God
himself.

The warfare of the gods, depicted by human art throughout long ages in a myriad of forms, is not in the main legendary. It is truly mythical; that is, mythically truthful. It
adumbrates man's experience of a central fact of the universe, the living universe, at once physical and spiritual, in
which we move and have our being. The gods when most
adored by men are not remote from the human struggle.
Because it is essentially *theirs*, they come down and take
part in it; and they fight all the more effectually because
they cannot lose their Peace. Deity is at once immanent and
transcendent, as theology puts it. Mythology, antecedently,
shows that the humane gods are "Sons" of the "Maker of
heaven and earth and of all things visible and invisible."
The Creator—Zeus, Brahma, or other—surpasses but in-

dwells his creation. He indwells it surpassingly in the persons of his divine-human Sons. Apollo and Vishnu, just because they are so richly human, are seen to be great impersonations of that which made and is ever making man. The Maker, in human and personal forms, toils and suffers with and for his creatures. Only when this is seen to be the necessity of his nature, is He vitally adored as the supreme Creator. And the divine mystery of immanent transcendence, though above our reason, *is within our dramatic experience.* We admire a great dramatist for creating living characters distinct from his own; yet he can only do so, we say, by "putting himself into his work." We recognize him as a transcendent artist because he is so vitally immanent. And thus we think of Deity when our thinking is normal; that is, mythodramatic.

Only the mythological imagination, not the Shakespearean, can be supremely dramatic. Certainly Shakespeare is more genial, in the civic sense, than the seers who wrote the Bible. He is more artistic; but also he is more artful. The Bible is more natural than his works, more true to life as a whole, more essentially dramatic. The drama of human life is real only because the universe is essentially a drama, as all great mythopoets have known. But those who wrote the Bible knew far better than any others how dramatic, in the highest sense, the very God himself is—how concerned with the human moral struggle, how immanent in history, how revelatory of himself in particular scenes and actions. . . . The unique revelation of the heart of Deity in Jesus Christ is not less sublime when it is seen to be entirely normal and natural from the standpoint of man's mythological intellect.

§4

But of course the Incarnation does not appear normal and natural from the standpoint of the purely academic mind.[3] It appears either miraculous in the sense of divinely law-breaking, or else utterly legendary. At the first it was a wild legend invented by ignorant people—a "stumblingblock" and a "foolishness" in the words of St. Paul—to the ancient intellectuals. But when they finally accepted it they viewed it as miraculous (i.e., lawbreaking). The theory arose that the nature of Jesus was different *metaphysically* from that of other men. But not the most elaborate Christological reasonings could reconcile that theory with the deep conviction of the writers of the New Testament that, though "without sin," He "was in all points tempted like as we are." He could not be the savior of human beings if He were at any point nonhuman. Therefore that notion, officially condemned by the Church, was bound to collapse in time, making room again for the other academic extreme, the theory that the central historic fact of Christianity belongs to the realm of legend. The increasing vogue of this

[3] The late Professor Charles A. Bennet makes a charming confession in his book, *A Philosophical Study of Mysticism* (New Haven, 1923), p. 87: "I have to confess to a certain prejudice. . . . I do not like the idea of a God who unbends to me personally. There is something stuffy and provincial in the thought that *my* salvation is important in the scheme of things. This, after all, is a Republican Deity, ready to shake hands with the humblest citizen and call him by name. He lacks a necessary dimension of Godhead, some of the Olympian remoteness and mystery of the Aristotelian Deity who did not condescend to notice the world and its affairs, but who drew the world after him not by what he did but by what he was. Of him one can say with Spinoza, 'Whoso loves God must not expect God to love him in return.' Yet . . . " Here the author proceeds to criticize effectually the point of view just given. The beauty and importance of his book derive from the fact that it comprises and yet, at its best, rises above the academic attitude.

theory during the past two hundred years was due to the advancing sway of secular academic thought.

Man has been called all sorts of an animal, a toolmaking, a laughing, a political, a religious animal. Not until today, however, has he thoroughy earned the title of Academic Biped. Our age will probably be termed by future historians "The Academic Age." Now, as never before, man is regarding the universe through academic spectacles. His eyes are commonly armed with big, round, celluloid-rimmed glasses; even Mr. Gandhi wears them. (On second thought, let's substitute "of course" for "even.") And this abnormal phenomenon has come to seem to us quite natural. Surely it will be abolished in the future by a humaner optical science which will discover how to develop our natural eyes instead of fitting them with bulging windows. But meanwhile many of us have to wear spectacles; and all of us have to look through them, more or less. Men, women, and children search the latest books and articles for the latest theories upon all aspects of life and the universe. The dramatic realities of business, politics, art, and religion are seen out of focus because they are viewed through the medium of academic concepts. Our ruling caste is the "professor," in the widest denotation of this word. It comprises the man in the street, who used to be so practical in contrast with the collegian, but who so often nowadays outprofessors the professor. And note that the word "expert," which used to mean a man who makes things work, means now a person who makes unworkable theories.

The worst delusions are in two fields, the economic and the religious, since these affect our daily bread, physical and spiritual. The notion that man can be saved mainly by attending to economic laws (which do not *humanly* exist) is a very bad error. But a worse one is the belief that man cannot be saved unless he severs religion from its anthropo-morphic basis. An American scientist fancied that he was doing just this, no doubt, when he declared at a recent meeting that "reverent science refuses to attribute any hu-man qualities to God." But clearly the speaker was creating God in his own image. He was interpreting the divine mind in terms of the mentality of a natural scientist; who arrives at a certain valuable but limited kind of truth by excluding from "Nature" all specifically human qualities. He was therefore exemplifying the truth of Voltaire's great epi-gram, even while trying to leave it behind. It is a law of Nature, of Complete Nature, that God must make man in his own image and that man must return the compliment. But the compliment is a very poor one indeed when we fashion our image of him by means of a limited part of our own limited intellect. In our current academic atmosphere, Deity, at best, is the Supreme Professorial Mind. Of course It excludes all possibility of the event that occasioned the Christian doctrine of the Incarnation. For that sort of event does not occur—it is a thing that "simply is not done"—in the best divine academic circles!

To be sure the term "Incarnation" is itself more or less academic. So were the early Christian thinkers who for-mulated the great dogma. Dogmas and councils, even the most inspired, are by nature academic. But the more we stress that fact, the more must we be awed by the way in which the academicism of the Catholic Councils of the Church was overtopped by true intuition. All the ancient alluring metaphysical theories about the nature of Christ yielded to the perception of his complete humanity. The formula of the Council of Chalcedon, "perfect God, per-fect man," is the bold assertion of a mystery beyond the reach of academic thinking. But of course that formula is subservient to the sublime prologue of the Gospel of St. John. Here, too, there is what may be termed an academic concept, that of the Word. But it is the greatest of concepts and it is entirely transfigured by the glory of supreme inspiration. The Word, the Logos, becomes mythological in the highest signification of that term. Therefore this prologue is recognized as the most effectual attempt so far to put into words the main meaning of the drama of the universe. The author sees, as none other, "eternity in an hour." He knows the uniqueness of the advent of the Christ because he knows how fully and naturally it accords with the way of Universal Life. "That was the true Light which lighteth every man that cometh into the world."

Alongside that passage, the recent pronouncement which I quoted earlier, "reverent science refuses to attribute any human qualities to God," appears indeed terribly academic. And such in general is the fate of modern "natural theology," as it is called. In fact, it is not very natural: it is not true to Complete Nature. It envisages only that aspect of nature which has been so wonderfully exploited during our era. Hence today the word "supernatural" commonly means "unnatural." It ought to denote that which is superlatively natural; just as "super-gasoline" means, I trust, the highest and purest form of that great modern motive power. The truth is that "natural theology" is far less natural than Christian theology. It is thoroughly academic. And a blatant paradox of our Academic Era, from the time of Edward Gibbon to the time of H. G. Wells, is the ridicule that has been showered upon the ancient councils of the Church as merely academic. Those ancient councils, unlike the counsels of Mr. Wells, were in the main practical. They had firm hold of a supreme historic fact and of the most practical function of the human mind, the mythological imagination.

To be sure the findings of that great faculty need to be continually revised by academic reason. The child's mythology is crude. The youth reacts from it, becoming an academician. The man, normally, regains the mythic truth of his childhood in purer form. But this third stage has been heavily hindered in the modern era. For academic reason, not content with its valuable secondary role in the drama of human thought, has essayed the leading part; the "professor" has played the "hero"! The academic mind has tried not just to criticize but to supersede mythology. As a result the philosophizing of our era has on the whole an air of juvenility. It is delightfully energetic, experimental, loquacious; but it is conceited and narrow, appallingly divorced from tradition, from total human experience. It does not see what the child sees nor know what the man knows. It has been immensely preoccupied with the youthful query, "*How* does man know—how *can* he know Reality?" (The answer is, he cannot if you rule out mythology.) It is scornful of those who modernly accept the Christian revelation: they are "obscurantists." This is a term which proud "enlightened" youths love to apply to their elders. It is a word dear to academic juvenility.

The worst of obscurations, however, is the refusal to recognize the dramatic nature of Reality. This refusal was avoided by the two greatest of Occidental academics: by Plato, because of his vital feeling for mythology; and by St. Thomas, because of his adoration of Christ. But it is a refusal that must always be made by purely academic thought, since this is by nature averse from Life Dramatic. The academic mind—Aristotle's, for instance—always tends to center reality in the contemplative intellect, in that which is aloof from the drama of persons and history. Hence personal and historic revelations of God must always appear to the strictly academic thinker either legendary or, if true, lawbreaking. For they are dramatic: they disturb the even tenor of the academic way.

Happily, however, there are plenty of signs that the Academic Era is beginning to draw to a close. The factors that brought it about have begun to reverse themselves. The chief factor was the disastrous schism in the Church four centuries ago. If the Church had reformed itself without losing its unity—its unity of spirit—Christian thought could have continued to be catholic, expanding itself to comprehend the results of modern science. Such expansion was forestalled by the militant sectarianism of the sixteenth and seventeenth centuries, with its retrospective theological and ecclesiastical hairsplittings. As a result the mythological imagination, pagan as well as Christian, was discredited; was regarded as poetic fume, not as the vehicle of Truth; so that for the majority of so-called "civilized" persons today the word "mythical" is synonymous with "untrue." Thus the ground was made ready for the monstrous mushroom notion of the eighteenth and nineteenth centuries that the method of natural science was the key to universal truth. However, that belief has now been undermined by natural science itself. And the science of theology is becoming vital again. It is redeveloping the capacity that it had in the thirteenth century for fusing old and new discoveries of the Divine Life. And sectarianism is abating. Some sort of confederation of the branches of the Church, a prospect that seemed Utopian a hundred years ago, is now well within the bounds of distant future possibility.

And philosophy today is not only freeing itself from naturalistic epistemology: it is becoming keenly aware of the inadequacy of concepts as interpreters of reality. Concepts may clarify life but they cannot render it. They need to be plunged again, so the phrase now runs, "in the full *stream* of vital experience." But a stream, as noted in the second part of this chapter, is a very partial image of life; it is essentially nondramatic. And the present popularity of this image is the consequence of a nondramatic era. William James was certainly a dramatically animated person. But the full stream of experience in which he strove to plunge philosophic thought, appears less and less dramatic as time goes on: it wears a late-Bostonian air. What is needed at present is the recognition that not just academic *thought* but academic *thinking* is an abstraction. It is a partial process detached from the mind's complete process; which, whatever else it is, is always dramatic and mythological. In other words, philosophy can become truly "pragmatic," not by plunging into *current* experience, but by striving to envisage the plot of the whole drama of life from the beginning until now. Which means that philosophy, if it is to find that fresh vitality for which it is now ardently groping, must become again subordinate to theology and mythology. And indeed this condition is actually being fulfilled by certain outstanding philosophers of the present time, whose influence will after a while become widespread. They have humbled themselves before great human tradition. They have recognized two facts that academic philosophy in itself cannot apprehend: the general fact that perfect humanity and divine perfection cannot be disjoined; and the particular fact that, after long natural and historical preparation, the eternal God was possessed completely of the will, the intrinsic being, of one completely human person. In him God became *the* Son of Man.

Thus the deadly division instituted by the Academic Era

between philosophy and religion is beginning to be healed. There may be again, in the future, a Catholic Council of the Church attended and much aided by the leading philosophers of the time—otherwise, of course, the council would not be entirely catholic. We may expect a gradual reconstruction of the mythodramatic view of life, in a broader and more reasonable form, we may hope, than that which was prevalent in the fifteenth century after Christ, not to speak of the fifteenth century before Christ. We may hope for the diffusion of a mental atmosphere in which the Holy Incarnation—the fact behind and above the dogmas of all Catholic Councils, past and future—will again appear divinely natural to the large majority of sane mundane persons. The man in the street will then be relieved from his present conscientious nightmare of religious academicism. Whether he will therefore be more moral, in the strict sense of that word, is beside the present question. The point is, he will be very much more human. . . . In the fish story with which I began, the younger of the two speakers was an objectionable mental prig. Whereas Moses, in spite of his crudities, was in the main normal and true to Complete Nature. In short, he was—in a phrase from current American slang—"the right sort of fish."

I turn next to a great man whose chief limitation as thinker and writer may be said to be this: while he very much desired be to wholly unacademic, he shared the essentially nondramatic view of life characteristic of the Academic Era. A more familiar name for that interesting phase of human history is the Romantic Era. In fact, it was at once academic and romantic; and so, to some extent, was Emerson; but not in his heart of hearts.

7.

Emerson's "Grace" *and* "Self-Reliance"

IN THE YEAR 1928 A KIND ACQUAINTANCE CONNECTED WITH the Emerson family conducted me through the great man's house in Concord. His library was the chief attraction. We lingered there for a long while, extracting from the shelves one book after another, at random but carefully, reverently. I could easily imagine the sage himself thus engaged in a leisure hour. From my youth on I had studied every picture and every written description of him that I could come at; and whenever I chanced to meet older persons who had actually seen him, perhaps even talked with him, I tried their patience with cross-examining questions. Gradually my mind had acquired a vivid moving picture of him. So that now he himself seemed to be present, stepping from bookcase to bookcase, pulling out volumes at random as I was doing—but not at all with my air of reverence. No; the noble Shade contemplated these books with an air of genial tolerance. I could see his eye and finger running rapidly from page to page. He was "reading for lustres," as he put it. Books were "for idle moments." The "great soul that o'er him planned" did not set much store by books. . . . But, I reflected, could that "great soul" be the Universal Soul itself, which is the source of all great books, and treasures them up to a life beyond life—Milton's writings, for instance, which appear on yonder shelf? Or was that "great soul" just Emerson's great soul, or was it just the soul of Emerson, or—

My confused broodings were broken in upon by a sharp exclamation from my companion—not, of course, the great Shade but the flesh-and-blood bookloving friend who had brought me hither. He handed me a book that he had just opened. It was the first volume of *Milton's Prose Works, A Selection,* published in Boston, in 1826. On the inside front cover was written in Emerson's script his little poem called "Grace"; containing, however, a passage that does not appear in the poem as printed. Here was a find indeed! It was very probably the original manuscript of the poem. But, with scholarly wariness, I shall hereinafter refer to this valuable holograph as MPW, i.e., the version of "Grace" written by Emerson, at one time or another, in his copy of *Milton's Prose Works.*

The printed poem reads as follows:

How much, preventing God, how much I owe
To the defences thou hast round me set;
Example, custom, fear, occasion slow,—
These scornèd bondmen were my parapet.
I dare not peep over this parapet
To gauge with glance the roaring gulf below,
The depths of sin to which I had descended,
Had not these me against myself defended.

In MPW, following the third verse, are two lines that were afterwards dropped. They declare that the "defences" which the poet has just acknowledged to God—"example, custom, fear, occasion slow"—

Were props to my tottering conscience,
Hedges to my soul from Satan's creeping feet.[1]

[1] These two unpublished lines are used with the permission of Raymond Emerson, Esq.

Obviously these lines were done on the spur of the moment. They are supernumerary to the rhyme scheme of the poem, and their rhythm leaps out of its rather stilted pentameter. Also the "props" and "hedges" and "creeping feet" disrupt the metaphor, which, suggested by the word "defences" in the second verse of the poem, is resumed with the word "parapet" and roundly developed in the remaining verses. Therefore it was natural enough that the author should delete the two irregular lines when he struck the second heat. Yet they have a pungent immediacy of rhythm and image lacking in the rest of the poem; and they are important for the present-day student of the mind and art of Emerson at the close of the third decade of his life.

His editors point out that this poem is related in spirit to a passage in his *Journals*, October 2, 1832; and they state that it may have been written at any time during the period 1831–1833. My own feeling, abetted as will presently appear by the two newly discovered lines, which were of course unknown to Emerson's editors, is that he composed it at the close of that period by way of recollecting in tranquillity a number of experiences he had had during those crucial years. On December 25, 1832, some months after his break with his church in Boston, owing to his objection to the use of tangible elements in the Communion service, the young ex-pastor set sail for Europe. While traveling about on that continent, which seemed to him sadly lacking in the purest guidance of religion, he became very sharply conscious of what he owed to his New England upbringing. In Naples, which he termed "a vast city of corrupt men," he wrote the following in his journal for March 13, 1833:

"When I was at home and felt vaunty, I pestered the

good folks with insisting on discarding every motive but the highest. I said you need never act for example's sake; never give pledges etc. But I think now that we need all the advantages we can get, that our virtue wants all the crutches; that we must avail ourselves of our strength, and weakness, and want of appetite, and press of affairs, and of calculation, and of fear, as well as of the just and sublime considerations of the love of God and of self-respect. Not that any others will bear comparison with these, but because the temptations are so manifold and so subtle and assail archangels as well as coarser clay, that it will not do to spare any strength." [2]

The long third sentence reads like a prose version, I should think a preliminary version, of the poem "Grace"; in particular, the "crutches" of virtue recall the "props" of conscience in the two rejected verses. In the final sentence the "subtle" temptations that "assail archangels" may recall (to the supersubtle reader, at least) "Satan's creeping feet" in the poem. But my main point is that the passage as a whole provides a fuller parallel to "Grace" than any other single entry that I have so far noticed in the *Journals*. On the other hand this passage lacks the mood of intense, almost abrupt, conviction, that governs the poem and that appears in other journal entries, during this period, concerned with the same general theme. For example:

"But there is a capacity of virtue in us, and there is a capacity of vice to make your blood creep. [April 25, 1831]

"Don't trust man, great God, with more power than he has, until he has learned to use that little better. What a hell

---

[2] For permission to use quotations from Emerson's *Works* I am indebted to the Houghton Mifflin Company.

we should make of the world if we could do what we would! [January 20, 1832]

"Is not then all objective theology a discipline, an aid, to the immature intellect until it is equal to the truth, and can poise itself? Yet God forbid that I should one moment lose sight of his real eternal Being, of my own dependence, my nothingness whilst yet I dare hail the present deity at my heart." [August 19, 1832]

Such passages indicate the kind of harmonious conflict that was going on in Emerson during the perplexed years preceding and following the resignation of his pastorate (September, 1832). In academic terms, it was simply the battle between Tradition and Romantic individualism in which the era was engaged. But the word "battle" does not well apply to Emerson's case. He never recognized any fundamental hostility between the two combatants. Later on, at the call of what seemed to him a public need—and incidentally, I believe, because the conservatives had hurt his feelings (he does not admit this motive himself but it seems clear to me from an exhaustive study of the biographic material)—he was to proclaim a doctrine of Self-Reliance over against conventionalism. In the transitional period under consideration, however, self-reliance was not a formulated doctrine but a condition of his personal development. It was the effort of his impressible and slow-growing genius to "poise itself," as he suggests in the last journal entry quoted above, in the midst of the conflict of past and present.

He was anxious that both the old and the new ideas should have their full impact and proper effect upon him. On account of his confessed inaptitude for sustained reasoning, he could not bring the two "mighty opposites" together in an organic and inclusive philosophy. Simply, he opened his mind first on the one side and then on the other in quick succession. He strewed his journals with contradictory statements which he allowed to lie side by side in the faith that at some time, in some way or another, they would be reconciled in the "Soul."

That situation accounts for the composition of "Grace," and for the fact that its cast is quite unique in Emerson's poetry. The piece is a sharp condensation of one side of the twofold mood that swayed him during his transitional years. It is extraordinary in its praise of "example" and "custom" just because the author felt that in moments of impatience he was inclined to be extraordinarily unfair to "these scornèd bondmen." He was developing his self-assurance, with the aid of European Transcendentalism. At the same time he saw that Transcendental self-reliance was commonly deficient in real poise and elevation, and at worst was even liable, in the words of the poem, to fall into "depths of sin." He noted that, in the individual man, "the understanding speaks much, the passions much, the soul seldom" (*Journals*, August 19, 1832). Therefore—if I may put the matter with a flat clarity which Emerson did not use—the Divine Grace has two complementary modes of operation which we dare not divorce from each other: one, through the great moments of inward experience; the other, through the guidance of great tradition. We may fairly sum up Emerson's double mood at this time by bringing together a clause from the poem and a clause, already quoted, from his contemporary journal: "How much, preventing God, how much I owe to the defences thou hast round me set! . . . whilst yet I dare hail the present deity at my heart."

Emerson saw that his self-reliance was considerably due to his ancestors. He saw that a noble quality of self-trust is the outgrowth of a noble and *continuing* tradition. One must deeply regret, from the standpoint of subsequent American culture and art, that he did not proceed to develop this idea and to emphasize it in his public utterances. It kept recurring to him in private. At the height of his public advocacy of the new individualism he wrote in his journals strong acknowledgments of what he owed to his forebears and to his upbringing. For long he entertained the notion of composing a sort of biographic compendium that would show the significance of New England tradition in shaping a lofty and distinctive type of character. There are hints that at times he even felt that he ought to do something more on behalf of Christ! But he did not get around to these tasks; as his disciple Whitman did not get around to his proposed task of writing up the soul when he had finished the body. A great deterrent was his decisive clash with the conservatives. About a year after his "Divinity School Address" he noted in his journal: "*Reform.*—The past has baked my loaf, and in the strength of its bread I break up the old oven." [July 7, 1839] This obviously alludes, with jocular complacency, to his public attitude; it is characteristic of his new non-humble frame of mind as lecturer and essayist. It is a fair summary of his essay "Self-Reliance" which he was now engaged in composing.

That essay, in spite of its ringing power, is a curious anomaly. It urges the reader to be true to his own experience, but very considerably it is untrue to the experience of Emerson himself. It urges writers to be "original and not conventional." But its pages are strewn with individualistic exaggerations which, derived from current Romanticism and not from the central course of Emerson's own experience, are really conventional and not original. For example: "No law can be sacred to me but that of my own nature.

Good and bad are but names very readily transferable to that or this; the only right is what is after my own constitution; the only wrong what is against." Such rhetoric illustrates Emerson's contention that a man cannot write his best unless he is uttering his own deepest convictions. The essay as a whole is untrue to Emerson's deep conviction that there can be no real opposition between true self-trust and sound tradition; that Grace working through tradition defends a man against himself, as the poem puts it. To be sure, in the middle of the essay [3] the author tries to dissolve the egoism of Romantic self-reliance in deity. "To talk of reliance is a poor external way of speaking. Speak rather of that which relies because it works and lives . . . the aboriginal Self, on which a universal reliance may be grounded." But deity, or divine grace, is represented here as working only through "Spontaneity" and "Intuition" (thus capitalized by Emerson), not at all through the check exerted upon these by "custom" and "example" as in the poem— only through individual experience, not through racial experience; not through history if this be regarded, says he, as "anything more than a cheerful apologue and parable of my being and becoming." In brief, *the false antinomy between self-trust and tradition is established and made to take on a religious air.*

Nowadays, when naturistic individualism is obviously in its second childhood, we need to cut through Emerson's official doctrine of self-reliance, as I like to call it, to his deeper and more comprehensive conviction. The great sage himself, I am sure, would approve of this proceeding if he were aware of our present conditions and needs. The *word* tradition was off-color for him, as for so many of his successors. But in his total writings the thing itself, under va-

[3] Paragraphs 21 ff.

rious other denominations, is considered and approved to a degree that would astonish anyone who is familiar only with his canonized essays. A good book could be written on this subject, including an important chapter on Emerson's debt to Milton. At an early age Emerson was deeply engrossed in Milton's prose as well as his verse. Continual reflection upon his work and character is evidenced in the earlier volumes of the *Journals* and culminates in the strong and fine panegyric of Milton published in *The North American Review* for July, 1838, now included in *Natural History of the Intellect and Other Papers*. In this essay, though the word "tradition" is not used, and Milton's freedom and modernity are stressed, it is obvious that Milton was for Emerson the modern acme of the great tradition coming down from the Greek classics and the New Testament. The central thought of the essay is that Milton "added the genius of the Christian sanctity" to "antique heroism," and is therefore "identified in the mind with all select and holy images, with the supreme interests of the human race."

But in "Self-Reliance," written not long afterwards, Milton's "highest merit" is asserted to reside in the fact that he "set at naught books and traditions"! This violent hyperbole was apt for Emerson in his then mood, but absurdly inapt for Milton. A contrary assertion had been entered in the *Journals* a few years earlier: "Milton was too learned, though I hate to say it. It wrecked his originality. . . . Wordsworth is a more original poet than he." [August 17, 1834] This statement, unless we accept the thin modern denotation of the term "original poet," is entirely untrue. And it marks a significant crisis in the story of Emerson's inner development. Hitherto, generally speaking, he had in his journals rigorously depreciated Wordsworth's poetry in comparison with Milton's. But now he was taking the Romantic *vates* more and more into favor, putting up with the deficiencies of his art for the sake of his "originality" as a seer. The entry just quoted continues: "He [the poet] speaks by that right that he has somewhat yet unsaid to say." This adumbrates the practical problem which young Emerson, as a writer, was now facing. His multifarious genius wanted to say everything, and indeed was pretty well doing so in the journals. But as poet and essayist he was trying to concentrate upon "somewhat yet unsaid to say." In this process Wordsworth proved to be a very present help: he did much to concentrate Emerson's vision in the direction of naturistic individualism. His shaping influence was exerted upon Emerson's first book, *Nature,* which just as this time, with much difficulty, was beginning to assume publishable form.

In short, Wordsworth and Milton acted as two great and quite contrary influences in Emerson's maturing years. Wordsworth's "originality" was midwife to his doctrine of transcendent self-trust. Milton kept him in vital contact with the truth of tradition, and, over against Wordsworthian egotism, impressed him freshly with the profound meaning of the ancient doctrine of humility. Emerson was critical, though alas not thoroughly critical, of Romantic spiritual pride. In his essay on Milton his claim that "no man in these later ages, and few men ever, possessed so great a conception of the manly character" culminates on the thought of Milton's religious humility: "the fact that true greatness is a perfect humility is a revelation of Christianity which Milton well understood."

Hence I believe that the chief extraneous factor that inspired the poem "Grace" was Milton. The doctrines of humility and grace go hand in hand, of course, throughout his

writings, particularly the Latin treatise "On Christian Doctrine," the rediscovery and Englishing of which in the
1820's provided an acknowledged impetus for Emerson's
essay on him. The formal movement and imagery of
"Grace," so exceptional in Emerson's verse, are reminiscent
of the Miltonic or, at least, of the seventeenth-century
style.[4] Milton's sonnet "On being arrived to the Age of
Twenty-three" comes to my mind when I read "Grace."

I like to imagine that Emerson composed the poem on
returning from Europe with a renewed sense of what he
owed to the Puritan tradition. During the homeward jour-
ney he was reading Milton (*Journals*, September 16, 1833);
perhaps he had with him the *Prose Works* in the first volume of which the MPW version of the poem now stands
inscribed, as explained above. In his library I examined these
volumes and found underscored many passages of Milton
that no doubt struck Emerson as having some bearing upon
his own mission as a writer. His journals show that this
question was occupying him during the long and stormy
sea voyage (September 4 to October 9) with his literary
career looming uncertainly on the western horizon ahead.
How was he to help in providing that new expression, so
cryingly needed in Europe and America, of the "wonderful
congruities of the moral law of human nature"? [Septem-
ber 8] The present answer was simply that, if he was to
be enabled to put "the law" into new words, he must put
it anew into his life—after the great example of Milton. He
writes: "Milton describes himself in his letter to Diodati as
enamoured of moral perfection. He did not love it more
than I. That which I cannot yet declare has been my angel

[4] The poem was published in the *Dial*, January, 1842. It "had the infinite
honor done it," says Emerson, "of being quoted to Herbert" (i.e., attributed to George Herbert).

from childhood until now. It has separated me from men. It
has watered my pillow, it has driven sleep from my bed.
It has tortured me for my guilt. It has inspired me with
hope. It cannot be defeated by my defeats. It cannot be
questioned, though all the martyrs apostatize. It is always
the glory that shall be revealed." [September 17, 1833]
This beautiful and well-known passage shows its full significance only when read in its biographic context. Emerson
was at this time "*un Milton jeune et voyageant*" in a richer
sense than Arnold was to be, a few years later, in George
Sand's epigram. In Emerson's crucial period Milton was a
real presence to him—the main bastion in the "parapet"
commemorated in "Grace," the chief influence in shaping
his nobler self-trust. The thought of Milton was closely
interwoven with the fresh sense of divine grace, and of courage and humility, that came to him during his uneasy homeward voyage. At the beginning of it, he jotted in his journal, "Be clothed upon with humility." On the day before
landing in New York, he indited a beautiful prayer the
theme of which may be described as self-reliant humility. I
quote just two sentences: "May I rejoice in the Divine
Power and be humble. . . . May I be more thine, and so
more truly myself, every day I live." Settled again in New
England, with a fresh appreciation of the "props" and
"hedges" that had been set around his younger years—and
before he was caught up on the full tide of his public dis-
avowal of props and hedges on behalf of the rising generation [5]—he would be just in the mood to open a volume of
his beloved Milton and inscribe therein the devout lines on
"Grace."

[5] His "revolutionary" attitude, if so it may be called, is anticipated
in his sermon delivered in the Second Church soon after his return to
Boston. See J. E. Cabot's *Memoir*, pp. 209-14.

§2

But never did he succeed in sufficiently clearing his mind
as to the basic difference between the outlooks of Milton
and Wordsworth, or, more importantly, between the Divine Grace and naturalistic self-reliance.[6] Of course, this
sort of criticism of Emerson is resented by the old-time
Emersonian, who is far from extinct in my own breast, and
who likes to cry out: "Emerson is first and last a poet, as he
himself declared, and why on earth should he be blamed for
not constructing a tight system of philosophy and theology?" But this question begs the question. No sensible
person could blame Emerson for not going in for logical
systems of thought. The point is that he did not sufficiently
clear his mind to be a real poet—unless one believes with
certain poets of today that a real poet is one who does not
clear his mind at all. This current belief is considerably a
fruit of Emersonianism.

But be it noted that Emerson himself keenly deplored his
own deficiency of form in both verse and prose. The good
essay or the good poem demands on the part of the writer
a certain preliminary clearing of the mind, hard to define
as a process, but easily recognizable in the resulting work
of art. Emerson is not first-class either as poet or essayist in
the strict sense of these two terms. From beginning to end
he is mainly a diarist, a journalist; and a very great one indeed; a higher Montaigne. How very much better his essay
"Self-Reliance" would have been if only he had written it as
what it essentially is, a diarian confession, instead of making

[6] Emerson's relation to modern self-reliance is dealt with in my essay
on "The Pride of Modernity" in the symposium called *Humanism and
America* (Norman Foerster, *et al.*, New York, 1930); and the final
chapter of my book *The Cycle of Modern Poetry* (Princeton, 1929) is
concerned with the question of Milton and Wordsworth.

it into an oratorical adjuration. But like other leaders of the Romantic Movement he wanted to adjure, to orate, to preach; and especially in America, for the descendant of many ministers, the lure was terribly strong. He humorously remarked in one of his early letters to Carlyle that he (Emerson) apparently considered his message to the public to be of great importance because he was taking so much trouble to find out just what it was. He never found out, really; for a "message" has a kind of consistency that a diary does not need. And the paradox of Emerson as writer is this, that even while yearning for a loftier form than diary, he deprecated the kind of consistency without which a diarist cannot attain a loftier form.

And beneath that paradox, indeed at the very root of all Emerson's incoherencies, is his failure to discriminate firmly between Divine Grace, in which he always believed, and human self-reliance, which he came to believe divine. So it is, in essence, no doubt, though not in actuality. But Emerson, while sharply aware of the sad difference between the ideal and the actual, would not draw a clear line between the human actuality and the divine essence of self-reliance. For such a line is a moral line; and Emerson, like the other Romantics and more or less in reaction from the conventional eighteenth century, did not like moral lines: they seemed to him conventional. But of course there is a line between a conventional moral line and a real moral line! "Dear me," I hear the great Shade exclaim, "you are full of lines, little man!" That would be a right enough rejoinder to a mere critic on the part of a great diarist. But it does not represent the right attitude for a would-be prophet in preaching to his people, the young American people whom he was urging to grow up. One does not grow up by means of ebullient and indiscriminate self-trust; one remains immature. Emerson is on solid ground when he is content to diarize genially his self-reliance, but not when he preaches it loftily. He made a capital blunder for art, morals, and religion when he insisted loftily upon self-trust without insisting clearly upon the line between right and wrong self-trust.

Moreover, as a man he drew the lines that he would not draw in his books. Thus there was a bad gap between his way of life and his literary way. This phenomenon was characteristic of the Romantics; it may be called the Romantic Hiatus. But in Emerson's case it stands out greatly because as a man he was so great. It accounts for a certain lack of lifeblood in his writings which he himself felt and deplored, though he did not put his finger squarely on the cause of it. In his best diarian-jovial manner he wrote, what I have already quoted above: "The past has baked my loaf, and in the strength of its bread I break up the old oven." He broke up Puritanism with the strength he had derived from Puritanism. He left the pieces lying around, looking at them fondly. If only he could have rebuilt the oven in modern shape, his writing would have attained a higher form and a richer vitality. He would have supplied the new America with an entirely genuine bread of the spirit instead of the fast-risen loaves that produced, for instance, Whitman.

As a man, Emerson was clearly a theist; but his writings gave people just occasion to accuse him of pantheism. "A stupid noun," he commented. But there was a real obtuseness in his own theologic vision. As a writer he did not shape out clearly what may be called the higher theism; he reacted confusedly from the current conventional theism. He was pleased when a little girl said of his pantheistic poem on Brahma, "It just means God." But this good little girl, like Emerson himself, had been brought up a good theist. A little girl today, say a freshman in one of our most enlightened colleges, would probably say of that poem, "It just means that I must do whatever I feel like—fine!" Emerson did not feel like clearing his mind theologically. That process would not have necessitated his becoming the thing that he mocked at, a theologian. But it would have necessitated his sketching unmistakably in his essays the idea of God that he actually lived by. Thus he would have done what he above all others seemed destined to do: namely, to reshape theism so as to save it for modern literature.

But he was afraid of appearing to endorse conventional gods. Emerson's persistent fear of conventionalism, a fear not recognized by himself nor sufficiently by his biographers, was a potent factor in his work. His predecessor, Wordsworth, though a much smaller person, had a sturdier kind of individuality, supported, of course, by the assured tone of the old national culture of England. Emerson shared the personal incertainty of young America, which had begun its career as a separate nation only a quarter of a century before its greatest sage's birth. He shared its tendency to be extremely conventional and, by way of reaction, wildly individualistic. In his life Emerson was far more conventionally correct than Wordsworth; in his writings he exerted himself to be far less so. He had to overdo his individualism to make sure that he had it—despite Boston! It is a significant fact that in the eighteen-thirties and forties, when young Emerson was launching his attack against "a foolish consistency," old Wordsworth was completing a life that illustrated, considerably and quietly, the inconsistent consistency that the young man was preaching so loudly.

"I suppose no man can violate his nature," Emerson was asserting. "Fear never but you shall be consistent in whatever variety of actions, so they be each natural and honest in their hour." That was the way that Wordsworth had lived. He was a Christian in youth, nominally at least; a kind of pantheist in his thirties; and a convinced Churchman in later life. But so little did this sturdy northern Englishman care about formal consistency that, unlike Emerson, he did not feel much need of justifying his changes to himself, let alone to others. He did not need to talk about personal as distinguished from formal consistency, so inexpugnably did he have possession of it. In 1834, when Emerson was getting away from conventional Christianity, Wordsworth was writing the following:

> But who is innocent? By grace divine,
> Not otherwise, O Nature, we are thine.
>
> .   .   .   .
>
> Vain is the pleasure, a false calm the peace,
> If He, through whom alone our conflicts cease,
> Our virtuous hopes without relapse advance,
> Come not to speed the soul's deliverance.

He wrote the above serenely indifferent to the fact that the truth embodied in these flat verses contradicted flatly the vision of the "Lines Composed A Few Miles Above Tintern Abbey" thirty-five years earlier, wherein no "He" and no "grace divine" were admitted. Emerson, however, became during his thirties fixed for life in a spiritual attitude akin to, though highly overtopping, Wordsworth's Tintern-Abbey stage; yet this was inconsistent with the theistic truth which fed his nobly growing life as a man. In religion he was consistently inconsistent, while Wordsworth was more like what Emerson preached that a man should be, inconsistently consistent. One reason was that Emerson unlike Wordsworth continued throughout his life to be sub-consciously and extremely afraid of being conventional.

In other words Emerson, in his literary-religious attitude, never really grew up. However, Wordsworth in growing up lost his youthful verve; Emerson retained his till death. And just there lies his value: he is forever young. He will always be read by young persons, and by old ones who wish to keep their spirits from turning gray. Unlucky is the man who cannot adore Emerson in youth; unluckier still if he does not criticize him in maturity and then, in middle age, look lovingly into his writings again and again. In this third stage we pick and choose among Emerson's sentences. And we realize anew the great, the divine, fact about the art of letters, that only when a man writes truth can he write supremely; that only in so far as he writes truth will his words withstand the corrosion of the years.

For instance, the following, which captivated us when young, cannot now satisfy: "A man should learn to detect and watch that gleam of light which flashes across his mind from within, more than the lustre of the firmament of bards and sages." This has about it a certain forced and rhetorical air—because it erects a false antithesis even while pointing to a great truth. The same general truth is rendered perfectly by Robert Frost in the following lines:

> Our very life depends on everything's
> Recurring till we answer from within.

But Emerson, in spite of his subtle distinction of "light" and "lustre," throws into a wrong opposition two ways of enlightenment that belong together. Often the authentic inward *flash* comes to us when we are watching "the firmament of bards and sages," and this firmament is more worth watching than many, if not most, of the inward *gleams* of most of us. In the context, i.e., the opening paragraph of "Self-Reliance," the author exclaims, "Speak your latent conviction and it shall be the universal sense." This, of course, is oratorical sophistry, as addressed to persons in general. However, we may read it as what it essentially is, a jotting in the diary of a gifted young man suffering somewhat from an "inferiority complex" and urging himself to throw it off. In the next paragraph, however, our eye is caught by a sentence rendering the true kind of self-trust: "A man is relieved and gay when he has put his heart into his work and done his best; but what he has said or done otherwise shall give him no peace." This is perfect and permanent writing. We note that the rhythm of the prose is true; whereas that of the first passage quoted above is pseudo-poetical; and the movement of the second passage is alliteratively blatant. Thus does the great diarist, whose writing is simply his variable self on paper, inform us, veraciously and unconsciously, as to his varying degrees of truth. And thus do we in middle age browse about, picking and choosing, in the vast diary which his complete works are.

We may say that he now appears to us in five guises: we discount the prophet, half admire the orator, sympathize with the poet, love the diarist, and venerate the sage. In this connection we shall need to modify Arnold's dictum to the effect that Emerson is great, not as a writer, but as "the friend and aider of those who would live in the spirit." Here Arnold shows his unfortunate tendency, appearing also in his essays on Milton and Wordsworth, to separate unduly the thought and the style of the author under consideration. The style is properly the form of the thought; and particularly is this so in the case of Emerson. He lacks wholeness of thought; therefore as poet and essayist he is deficient in that wholeness of form which means perfect art. But Arnold's kind of classicism, which made him over-value Gray, caused him to undervalue the original and superb art of Emerson's sentences and sentence groups—his diarian art. Emerson is a far greater writer than many who are completer artists, including of course Arnold himself; I should include also Swift, whom, as writer, Arnold puts above Emerson. For Arnold, Swift was "among the great writers, the great men of letters"—but not Emerson! On the other hand, Arnold could not be truly critical of Emerson's confused Over-Soul, for this had contributed much to Arnold's own transcendent "power that makes for righteousness." To put the matter more precisely, and more lugubriously, Emerson's pantheistic Unitarian theism had helped Arnold to evolve his Anglican Stoic pantheism. . . . In short, Emerson is a much greater writer, and a much more dubious friend to those who would live in the spirit, than Arnold could see. And it is exactly when Emerson is at his best as a writer that he is most reliable as a spiritual guide, so veraciously revealing is his style.

When I was quite young I made my first pilgrimage to Emerson's grave. The day was overcast and bleak; I saw no living person in the large cemetery at Concord. Undirected I did not find for a long while what I was seeking. Then suddenly, in the midst of rows of conventional and mostly ugly tombstones, I came upon his great rock of unshaped granite. That was as it should be; so also, I then thought, was the inscription on it:

> The willing master lent his hand
> To the great soul that o'er him planned.

But when some years had gone by, that couplet, for me,
went by too: it seemed hopelessly sophistic and oratorical;
the word "planned" appeared strikingly inapposite. And
even now, I confess, I should like to see carved under that
epitaph two or three lines from his humble poem on
"Grace," to counteract its air of airy self-reliance. However, I now look through the words of that couplet and
take its good meaning, more fully than in younger days: it
means his radiance. Emerson, the most planless of the sages,
surpasses the others in a special personal radiance; which,
one feels mysteriously, could not have existed if there had
been *much* more plan in him. His light is not, in the main,
religious; until one sees that fact one cannot see the truth
of him. But he is a kind of divine joker in the pack of the
world's sages; for God, who is perfectly planful, did not
wish the game of human wisdom to be too smoothly
planned. So He created Emerson: He planned something,
at least, of Emerson's planlessness; and thus there is a certain rightness in that epitaph. A kind of ever-young Jovian
carelessness is perhaps the essence of Emerson's radiance.
. . . In the sacred precincts of his library in his house at
Concord, fingering his books with a reverence that he denied them, I had a renewed feeling of his exceptional presence—the nobility of stature, the free vigor of intellection,
the serene gleam, the *sentiment* divine.

8.

Notes on Civilization and Christianity

§1

THE HUMAN WAY

CRITICAL HUMANISM, AS EXEMPLIFIED IN *American Criticism*, by Professor Norman Foerster,[1] formerly a student of Irving Babbitt's, is clarified and heightened common sense. It is skeptical of all abstract theories as to the whence and whither of life, while, at its best, carefully respectful towards any deep intuitions into the nature of life that may be caught in the meshes of such theories. It is intensely interested in the question: *"How* may *human* life be lived most effectively and happily?" It is no more entranced by new physics than by old metaphysics. It notes that in old days atoms gave way to angels; that, after a while, angels gave way to atoms again; that, in our time, atoms have given way to electrons, and electrons are giving way to—God knows what—angels again, probably. (Of course I am here speaking of man's angels, not God's.) Electrons are swift, insubstantial, drenched with the mystery of light; they are "bright with something of angelic light."

Occidental spirituality, now thin but eager, may presently feed itself fat on angelic electrons, and, strutting to the center of the stage, proceed to recapture the leading role from materialism. Bertrand Russell, intimate with both

[1] *American Criticism,* A Study in Literary Theory from Poe to the Present. New York, 1928.

parties, announces that already "the death-blow has been given to materialism." But common sense yawns and doubts. That encounter has been staged so very often in the courts of human history. That "death-blow" is merely histrionic. Nowadays, perhaps, we have a special chance to perceive that the two actors are really a single protagonist, a quick-change artist who plays a double role, who divides himself (in Hotspur's phrase) and goes to buffets with himself. The material and the immaterial, the elements and the angels, are two aspects of nature. (See, for instance, Kipling's "Angel of the Off-shore Wind" in his superb *Last Chantey!*) There is no quarrel between them, except in our histrionic fancies. We are impelled to fancy such a quarrel because it gives us an image, though a faint and misleading image, of the conflict between the devil and the deity in our own proper nature.

"Practically, the rightful concern of man is his humanity, his world of value and quality that marks him off from a merely quantitative natural order," says Mr. Foerster. "In assuming this duality, humanism appeals to the authority of the actual experience of mankind, past and present. Of the trend of past experience there can be no doubt; both of the old guiding traditions, the Greek and the Christian, however different outwardly, were absolutely at one in their sharp contrast between the human and the natural. Scarcely more doubtful is the trend of present experience: even in an age when the official philosophy is monistic, the working philosophy of the vast majority of mankind is still dualistic. Men are still conscious of an inner conflict, insusceptible of reconciliation, between the expression of natural desire and the will to conform to a standard of values." Certainly this is the essential conflict; and such plain sight of it energizes common sense, freeing its eyes from the daz-

zle of the age-old shifting pageantry of naturistic theories
and sentiments. Naturism—the investigation of nature's elements and the worship of her spirits—has been dominant
enough during the past two centuries to obscure, disas-
trously, the real duality of man. The new critical humanism
is therefore placing a strong emphasis upon that duality.

Yet Mr. Foerster, author of *Nature in American Literature* and himself a keen and loving student of nature, is
carefully fair to naturism and brings out its positive values
for literature. He gives us a comprehensive and well-bal-
anced account of the views of Poe, Emerson, Lowell, and
Whitman regarding literature and its relation to life. Nothing could be fairer than his treatment of our most declarative poetic naturist, Walt Whitman. But especially fresh
and compelling is the essay on Lowell. Mr. Foerster shows
that "his weakness was the very reverse of that which is
commonly alleged; that, instead of having insignificant cri-
teria and effective personal qualities, he possessed a set of
controlling ideas that wanted only the impetus of great
personal qualities to make them in the highest degree significant and useful." The book as a whole, in addition to
being timely, is *the* authority on its subject. It is progressively interesting and convincing.

Sometimes its clarity is a bit superficial; notably in the
three final pages of the essay on Emerson. Here Mr. Foerster assimilates the great essayist—or diarist, as I prefer to
call him—to the great men of religion, including Jesus, and
says that his total view of art leaves us cold for the reason
that "his cast of mind was dominantly priestly rather than
poetic." But "priestly" is just the wrong word to apply to
Emerson. It should be "visionary"; as indeed Mr. Foerster
himself suggests in an earlier passage. "Emerson recoiled
from the natural man with something like horror. Yet he

believed—and herein was he the visionary—that the yawn-
ing chasm between the actual and the imagined could be
bridged, not by strenuous ethical work, but by the simple
expedient of self-reliance, i.e., reliance upon the influx of
spirit." I should say the important fact is that Emerson's
imagination, unlike the imagination of Jesus, of the greatest
poets, and of highly normal humanity, did not respond to
the moral strife which shapes, and even creates, what is
most precious in human personality. Emerson saw this conflict coolly with his mind, but he did not warm to it deeply
with his imagination. That is why common sense does not
warm to him, thoroughly, either as prophet or as poet.
That is why he is not at all a priest. And finally, that is
why his work, in spite of his wide love of the drama of
life, is at center extraordinarily nondramatic; as I suggested
at the close of the essay on "Life Dramatic" above.

Yet, as I have tried to show in the preceding chapter,
Emerson was a great humanist in the bent of his spirit,
though not in the ways of his "trackless mind." So Mr.
Foerster calls it; yet he also puts his finger on the humanist
in Emerson. "However responsive he may have been to the
romantic mood that still prevailed in his time, we are bound
to feel, the more we study him, that he was even more responsive to the spirit and doctrine of Christianity and of
Greek humanism." One of the best passages in the book is
the demonstration of Emerson's "recoil from the romantic
ego and attachment to what he terms the general mind of
man." He knew more greatly than his contemporaries that:
"Without aiming at morality, all great art emancipates us
from the egoistic self and elevates us to that universal self
wherein the fair and the good are one." Mr. Foerster's book
is a call for a new and firm vision of that truth today. In his
summary of the contemporary situation of American litera-

ture, creative and critical, he says: "The philosophy of humanism finds its master truth, not in men as they are (realism) or in men as worse than they are (naturalism) or in men as they wish to be (romanticism), but in men as they *ought* to be—'ought,' of course, not in the usual restrictedly moral sense, but with reference to the perfection of the human type."

§2

A CATASTROPHIC VIEW

"*Where there is no God there is no man:* that is what we have learned from experience". . . . "The ways of Humanism and the Renaissance have been fully explored. There is no longer any possibility of advance along them". . . . "The new man, indifferent to divine sanctions, wanted to be the maker and master of life without help from on high". . . . "Our own time, since it has pushed all the antinomies of life to their limits and has come to a knowledge of its own origins, begins to understand that there was a fatal mistake and abuse of itself in the assurance of Humanism, and that at the roots of its creed was hidden a virtual self-negation of man and of his fall. When he broke away from the spiritual moorings of his life he tore himself from the deeps and went to the surface; and he has become more and more superficial. When he lost the spiritual centre of Being, he lost his own at the same time."

These four passages, selected with some care from the earlier pages of Nicholas Berdyaev's *The End of Our Time*,[2] and arranged in my own order, give a summary of his essentially catastrophic view of our present civilization.

[2] Translated by Donald Atwater. London, 1933.

He attacks the popular notion that man and his world were repressed in the Middle Ages and fully discovered in the Renaissance. He claims that this discovery, begun of course in ancient times but lagging until it derived from Christ a divine completeness of motive, was most fully made by the medieval mind. And though, as everyone knows, the recapture of what was best in the ancient culture was essential, yet far more important, Berdyaev insists, was the stern education that the medieval spirit underwent between the decline of the Roman Empire and (say) the eleventh century. Those dark ages detached Western man from the vast material civilization that he had built up and prepared him to discover his true and full relation to Nature and to God.

At the height of the medieval vision, human society was seen to be "hierarchic" and "ontological." Every creature, every object in the universe, was recognized to be real and meaningful in its relation to Eternal Being and in that relation alone. Each person had his place in visible society because each soul had its place in the unseen Kingdom of God. And the facts of that Kingdom were bodied forth by "the authentic and holy things of the Catholic Church." Such were the conditions that made possible what we call the Renaissance but which, properly considered, was a second and lower wave of the great medieval renaissance. Shakespeare's work and all the other great achievements of that era were based upon the profound conception of human personality and human society attained by the medieval mind.

But the medieval church, untrue to its highest vision, had materialized itself into a theocratic imperialism, violating the freedom of souls essential to the Kingdom of God. Hence there rose in the Renaissance an unprecedented rage for freedom—not just from the Church but from the divine power which she so signally represented. Such is the root of the modern tragedy. We moderns have developed our amazing outward powers in revolt from our deepest inward power, the Divine Grace. Hence our society has lost its inner cohesions. The obverse of modern individualism is modern socialism, which attempts, like the medieval church at its worst, to force an outward and mechanical unity upon men. Our attempts to found society upon purely secular bases—national, democratic, socialistic—have become more and more Satanic. Their natural culmination is the Satanic religion of Communism in Russia.[3]

And now, Berdyaev believes, we are on the threshold of a new Dark Age which can lead us, as in medieval times, to a new age of light. The rhythm of history, which is essentially divine, has brought us again to that thorough disillusion with secularism which characterized the opening centuries of the Christian era. We must now leave behind us the "weary day of modern history." But "night is not less wonderful than day, it is equally the work of God; it is lit by the splendour of the stars and it reveals to us things that day does not know." In the times just ahead of us "the religion of Satan and the spirit of Antichrist must needs dominate quantitatively." They will be warred upon, however, by a renewed Christianity, freed from secular entanglements and able to save us again.

But what, one must ask just here, will prevent us from proceeding to duplicate the errors of the Middle Ages? For this question Berdyaev has no real answer. He says we must try to carry over into the new Dark Age our modern gains, in particular our freedom of conscience. But this is the achievement of that very Humanism which, he claims, has now lost all validity. Its "happy medium," its middle way

[3] Berdyaev was expelled from his country, Russia, in 1922.

between heaven and hell, has been tried and found impossible. In one passage the author says: "The nineteenth century saw the decomposition of Humanism by itself, the end of the Renaissance." In another passage: "The humanism of Feuerbach and Auguste Comte, apostles of the 'religion of humanity,' has almost nothing in common with that of the Renaissance." Surely it is rather rough on Humanism to make it responsible for that with which it *has almost nothing in common*. The trouble is that Berdyaev comprises in the term "Humanism" two opposed qualities. Certainly the Renaissance sowed the seeds of a false humanism, a "religion of humanity," better called humanitarianism. But it also revived a true Humanism, which has fought in recent years against the false variety, as it fought in the early days of the Renaissance against false and decadent priestcraft.

However, Berdyaev claims that all the positive values of true Humanism are derived from religion and that therefore Humanism is redundant. But even if his premiss were true his conclusion is false. The complete Christian, doubtless, is at the same time a true Humanist. But complete Christians are rare and Berdyaev himself, free from religionistic optimism, believes that they will be rare till the end of time. Meanwhile, then, a sound ethical Humanism can be useful. It will serve as a standard and a way of life which Christianity must ever strive to include and to transcend. Without it, the Dark Age that the author says we are entering will be dark indeed, the prey of religious sentimentalism and obscurantism.

But Berdyaev's writing has a seer-like quality that shines above its confusion of thought and its tossing repetitiousness of style. The agony of Russia is there and the mounting of a fine soul through and above that agony to a fresh vision of faith, hope, patience, and charity. A blessed relief it is to turn from the current literature of sickly disillusion to a book wherein the true disillusion is shown. Berdyaev is disillusioned in regard to human knowledge and human freedom, and even in regard to the symbolism which he loves and uses. He writes: "I cannot any longer realize the ends of knowledge without adverting to religion and undergoing a religious initiation into the mysteries of Being." . . . "Not for anything in the world would I be free from God: I wish to be free *in* God and *for* God." . . . "What is needed is not to spread ourselves abroad, to display the signs and symbols of an interior life, but to steep ourselves in true spirituality, to come back to the fatherland of the spirit." That is, symbols must be used vitally.

§3

PROGRESS AND THE MIDDLE AGES

The movement called the Enlightenment, growing out from the Renaissance and culminating in the eighteenth century but still widely alive today in its multifarious aftereffects, has for its reverse side the *Endarkenment* of the modern mind in its attitude towards the Middle Ages. Those two phenomena are two sides of one thing. Without the Endarkenment as background, there would have been in the foreground a notable luminescence, indeed, but not *the* Enlightenment. If it had not been for the modern break with the medieval mind, the rejection of it as irrational and darkly unprogressive, modern rationalism could not possibly have seemed brightly rational nor modern progressivism wonderfully progressive. The immense submission of philosophy during the past three centuries to the concepts and methods of physical science—surely an outstanding episode in the history of human superstition—could not have appeared enlightened if the meaning of thirteenth-century thought had not become fully endarkened.

Accordingly, the lightening of the Endarkenment has proceeded in equal pace, since the end of the eighteenth century, with the darkening of the Enlightenment. The latter has descended stage by stage from the Wits of the aristocratic age to the populace, and to populace-minded writers, of the present time: it has sunk from a flare of select spirits to a "gloomy light much like a shade" of widespread dying embers. For the beacons of the Enlightenment turned out to be mainly brilliant bonfires. After usefully destroying much accumulated rubbish, they bequeathed to the nineteenth century a sinking spiritual twilight. Already, however, the rediscovery of the Middle Ages had begun. The history of this movement will some day be written, from its first Romantic gropings to its culmination in (perhaps) the twenty-first century. But if the story is fully told it will have to be two-sided. It will show the descent of Rationalism from Hume, let's say, to Professor Dewey and Earl (Bertrand) Russell, and the rise of spiritual reason from the shadowy haze of Coleridge to the daylight of A. E. Taylor, Von Hügel, and Maritain.

Among the distinguished thinkers who in the twentieth century are retrieving the meaning of the Middle Ages with a fullness of enlightenment not possible before, the Roman Catholic historian, Christopher Dawson, if not the most powerful and penetrating, is the most comprehensive and, to use a popular term, the most "social-minded." Competent in many fields of learning, he brings all his knowledge to bear on the problem of society: he studies the origin and growth, the values, sins, and prospects, of Occidental culture. And for him the chief crisis in the plot of the whole complex drama occurs in the height of the Middle Ages; i.e., the period from the tenth to the thirteenth century. For it was just then, he claims, and not under the Roman Empire, that Europe first became Europe. It was only then that she achieved a cultural pattern sufficiently comprehensive to bring into fruitful co-operation all her great inheritances, racial, political, religious, and intellectual. And though that harmony was transient in its outward form, the lesson of subsequent history, according to Mr. Dawson, is that the essentials of the medieval pattern must now be restudied, resumed, and carried on if Europe is again to achieve anything like a real unity. The extraordinary vitality of Europe in the past four centuries, the very energy which has produced those assertive sectional interests which now threaten to destroy or debase her civilization, was generated by *Europe as a society*, and can be maintained and controlled only if that society is reconstituted in modern form.

In Mr. Dawson's *Mediaeval Religion and Other Essays*,[4] consisting of six essays on various aspects of medieval culture, he makes clear that the Middle Ages, so far from being "the ages of Faith in the sense of unquestioning submission to authority and blind obedience," were a period of spiritual struggle and incessant mental and social change. The restoration of contact with the main tradition of Greek thought—which had been lost in the Dark Ages, not through the working of Christianity but because of the internal decay of Roman civilization—is not only one of the chief medieval achievements: "It is a turning-point in the history of world civilization, for it marks the passing of the age-long supremacy of Oriental and eastern-Mediterranean culture and the beginning of the intellectual leader-

[4] New York, 1934.

ship of the West." The quick absorption by the West of Graeco-Arabic science in the twelfth and thirteenth centuries is an extraordinary event. The "modern errors" of the new thinkers were loudly condemned by traditionalists and there was a real danger that Western culture would be sacrificed, like the culture of Islam, to a conflict between theology and science. This was prevented, however, by "the eagerness and intellectual courage" of the contemporary leaders of Christian thought.

But Mr. Dawson knows that the greatest achievement of the Middle Ages was not intellectual synthesis, much less ecclesiastical organization: it was a "deepening of the spiritual life by a new type of religious experience." This grew out from a fusion of the lofty mysticism of the East with Western religious humanism and found its concrete expression in what may be called, as the author says, "the passion of the humanity of Christ." This acme of the medieval cultural harmony is all too briefly treated by the author. And the reader is surprised to find him declaring in his chapter on "The Romantic Tradition" that if we wish to find "the quintessence of the medieval spirit, we cannot do better than to follow the example of the modern Romantics and look for it in the age and country of the Troubadours." He shows elsewhere that the courtly idealism of the Troubadours, Arabic in its origin, was essentially materialistic and anti-religious in its spirit; which medieval Christianity, by reason of its catholic scope, was able to attach and to transmute in a manner that looks miraculous. Why, then, call the Provençal idealism "the quintessence of the medieval spirit"? Apparently because Mr. Dawson is here anxious to demonstrate that "the rediscovery of the Middle Ages by the Romantics is an event of no less importance in the history of European *thought* [the italics are mine] than the rediscovery of Hellenism by the Humanists" of the Renaissance. However, his book culminates in an excellent essay on *The Vision of Piers Plowman*, a poem deeply typical of the Middle Ages just because it is dominated by "the passion of the humanity of Christ." Mr. Dawson does not say, but he leads one to say, that that religious experience, reanimated in modern form and again guiding philosophy, would be the chief light to enlighten our darkened Enlightenment.

The Enlightenment, though rooted in the Renaissance, grew rapidly away from the best spirit of that period. There is a deep gulf between the Cartesian rationalism and that catholic philosophy, achieved in the Middle Ages but not fully and imaginationally humanized then, which underlies the great art of the Renaissance—the poetry, for instance, of Spenser, Shakespeare, and Milton. Now, in various passages of Mr. Dawson's works he shows a disposition to deny the distinctiveness of Renaissance humanism, to merge it into the rationalistic humanitarianism which was its bastard offspring. To lose the spirit of the Renaissance in regaining that of the Middle Ages would be most unfortunate. And the root of the trouble (it plainly appears in *Mediaeval Religion*) is that he has not yet discerned a thoroughly *internal* cause of the decline of the medieval harmony as distinct from subsidiary factors—a deficiency comparable with those inherent causes of decline which in his previous books he discovered in previous civilizations. Consequently in his view the medieval culture seems so very exceptional that it quite overshadows the Renaissance, wherein the sources of decline are very patent to him. But fortunately Mr. Dawson's thought is still in process of development and may

later fill in its lacunae. And this book is packed with vital
facts and ideas which Americans, in particular, stand very
much in need of.

In another book [5] Mr. Dawson says, "It may seem paradoxical to suggest that the starting-point of human progress
is to be found in the highest type of knowledge—the intuition of pure being; but it must be remembered that intellectually, at least, man's development is not so much from the
lower to the higher as from the confused to the distinct."
This statement, from the current sociological standpoint, is
revolutionary. But the author backs it up with a firm array
of facts. The *essence* of primitive religion is not a belief in
ghosts or magic or totem. It is not animism or pantheism
or polytheism. It is "an obscure and confused intuition of
transcendent being." When this intuition has been educated
by long eras of experience and by great centuries of culture
it becomes, as in Plato and St. Thomas Aquinas, the clear
summit of human knowledge. But from the first it is present, since human nature in all times is radically the same,
and it is the ultimate motive of human progress.

This intuition gave rise to Shamanism. The Shaman or
primitive Messiah was venerated by the tribe, not primarily
as a magician and not at all as the representative of a particular god, but, above all, as a person peculiarly in touch
with supernatural life and being. He was succeeded by the
organized priesthood and the elaborate myths of the cults
of fertility. This cultus may well have been the originator,
as it was certainly the inspirer and director, of the art of
agriculture, the *sine qua non* of human civilization. Each of
the great archaic cultures, from the Egyptian to the Mayan,
consisted of a ritual order based upon the agricultural year

[5] *Progress and Religion*. London, 1929.

and embracing the whole life of society. The ritual order
was a reflection of the cosmic order on the one hand and,
on the other, it was man's organized effort to master his en-
vironment, physically and spiritually. It was thus that man
found his true position and purpose between the heavens
and the earth.

In the archaic cultures the sense of transcendent being
was by no means lost, though obscured, and it was brought
again to the foreground by the great religions and religious
philosophies that rose in southeastern Europe and southern
Asia during the first millennium B.C.—Platonism, Judaism,
Buddhism, Confucianism. They represent "a change of
thought rather than a revolution of material culture," and
they "have laid a permanent foundation on which our own
intellectual and religious tradition is based." For Christianity emerges from that wonderful period as the chief synthesis and fulfillment of its efforts, drawing together the
genius of Europe and the genius of Asia. Broadly speaking,
Asia has always tended to lose Nature in the search for God
while Europe has tended to lose God in the search of Nature. But Judaism, rising in the borderland between the two
continents, conceived of God as indeed transcendent and
yet as working out his purposes through human nature and
human history. This conception was carried on and developed by Latin Christianity. The "world process" was seen
to be a "divine drama." And "the Absolute and the Finite,
the Eternal and the Temporal, God and the World were
no longer conceived as standing over against one another
in mutual isolation. The two orders interpenetrated each
other; and even the lower world of matter and sense was
capable of becoming the vehicle and channel of the divine
life." Hence Christianity, aided by Greek thought, could
embody "a genuine spirit of humanism." And the great

Catholic synthesis of the thirteenth century was animated by "the desire to show the concordance in difference of the two orders." Aquinas, emphasizing "the autonomous character of natural activity, the province of Reason as distinct from that of Faith, the moral law of Nature as distinct from that of Grace, the rights of the State as distinct from those of the Church," laid the mental ground-lines of modern civilization.

The modern doctrine of progress, first clearly formulated by the Abbé de St. Pierre in the early eighteenth century, is a narrow and debased offshoot from Catholic teleology. Inspired by the Christian belief in the high destiny of man, it was able to obtain a wide hold upon Occidental society, conjoining sentimental and mechanistic elements that in themselves are hopelessly contradictory and instable. Today it is clear that "the religion of progress" has run the full gamut of its limited possibilities. Meanwhile it has brought about an abnormal and unprecedented secularization of culture, so that Occidental society has well-nigh lost its inner cohesion.

"Since a culture is essentially a spiritual community," says Mr. Dawson, "it transcends the economic and political orders. It finds its appropriate organ not in a State but in a Church, that is to say a society which is the embodiment of a purely spiritual tradition and which rests, not on material power, but on the free adhesion of the individual mind." At the same time the "church" must exert a fostering and controlling influence upon the other "orders." And just as the archaic "churches" were designed to exert that influence upon agriculture, so Christianity was designed to exert it upon the modern utilization of Nature. "For the progressive intellectualization of the material world which is the work of European science is analogous and complementary to the progressive spiritualization of human nature which is the function of the Christian religion. The future of humanity depends upon the harmony and co-ordination of these two processes. . . ." In short, the "religion of progress" needs to be reabsorbed and repurified in the religion of Christ. Occidental society can be really reintegrated only through the Church which created it—that is, traditional Western Christianity.

Unfortunately, however, the great religious schism of the sixteenth century resulted in Christianity's becoming sectarianized and culturally impoverished. And Mr. Dawson's treatment of that fact is quite inadequate. In dealing with the archaic and ancient cultures, he points out that at the very height of their ritual order and intellectual achievement they began to decline through *a failure of moral vitality*. But he omits this consideration when he comes to the decline of medieval culture after the thirteenth century. He passes over that decline. A frank criticism of Roman as well as of Protestant Christianity would have strengthened the total effect of his book. So would a consideration of the efforts of recent theologians on both sides of the line to redefine the Christian "revelation" in a sense at once Catholic and sublimely "natural." That frank criticism and that redefinition are pre-essential to the reunion of Christendom.

So also is the effort that is now being made for a distinct revival of humanistic ethical standards. But Mr. Dawson consistently underestimates the value of ethics as distinct from religion; for example, in his treatment of classic Buddhism and Confucianism. He intimates that one who values "the active moral life as an end in itself" is "an Americanist." But alas, the "Americanist" cannot fully deserve this ironic tribute unless the word "moral" be omitted from it. Moreover, the "Americanist" values the active life—outward work—not as "an end in itself" but for the sake of emotional excitement and the sense of material power. Whereas the new American academic humanism is advocating inward work, not as "an end in itself," but for the sake of temperate happiness and the sense of peace. . . . From Mr. Dawson's view of the philosophy of Aquinas, cited above, it would seem to follow that, in succession to the reign of scientific naturalism, a distinct revival of "the moral law of Nature" would now be in order. Without such a revival, the Catholic Christianity of the future which Mr. Dawson hopes for would not be adequately catholic.

However, his book is important and interesting. It is an extraordinarily compressed, clear, and vivid story of human civilization. Its distinction is that its thesis, our rising need of traditional Christianity, is based not on pious conviction but on sociological principles and wide-ranging investigation. Its attitude, apart from the limitations noted, is remarkably catholic.

§4

CULTURE AND EVANGELISM [6]

Readers who have not yet looked into any of the dozen volumes already published by the Reverend Dr. Hough may find his present book an effective medium for making his acquaintance. It is brief, comprehensive, alluringly concrete, and remarkably climactic. One may say it begins with Glasgow and ends with Jersusalem the Golden. Considering the title of the book the first of its five chapters may strike the reader as pleasantly superficial, and I think it is indeed somewhat too "literary." But soon one finds that it is an

[6] Harold Lynn Hough, *The Great Evangel*. Nashville (Tenn.), 1936.

integral part of the author's whole plan. It pictures the murkinesses of industrial cities while it hints at an ever present Light—in such a way as to lend full point to its closing sentence: "There is no spot in which a human being finds himself from which there is not a straight road to the City of God." And that road is pursued through the remaining chapters, which form an ascending series showing the appeal of the Christian gospel to the Mind, the Conscience, the Heart, and the Whole Life.

The second and third chapters may be considered together. The author urges that today "true evangelism" must be "intelligence on fire." The modern mind needs to be and can be convinced that Christianity has in it the most "coherent interpretation of the universe and life." *Intelligence* can learn that "God must be the great sufferer as well as the complete intelligence." Here one expects the author to give his own exploration of Incarnational philosophy. But he does not do this; nor does he render an adequate account of what may be called non-Christian moral happiness. No doubt he considered those two topics too large for such a short book. But he develops convincingly the following truth: "The very structure of moral personality sets processes in motion which must at last find their fruition in religion that transcends morality at the very moment when it fulfills all its high behests." In passing, he makes sharp criticisms of false religiosities, such as "the subtle aesthetic pleasure of being altruistic"; and finally he brings out "the gay zest" which belongs to the true faith.

The fourth chapter, in which the theme culminates, is nothing short of masterly. Let the cultivated reader who shrinks from an essay entitled "The Evangel which Wins the Heart"—let him read this chapter. Here he may find a culture richer than his own; a happy art of combining informality with firm form; and, more deeply interfused, an authentic fire. Read for instance the allegory, early in this chapter, of the "Christ of hate"—the kind of Christ that the purest and loftiest man of men would have become if, after fathoming with unique insight all the wickedness of a world that was rejecting him, had in the end rejected it, supernally hating its ways. As for the real Christ: "There was not enough wickedness in the world to take the love out of his heart and to put hate in its place. . . ." Towards the end of the chapter "the deathless splendor of love which saves the world" is illustrated by a homely incident (too sacred to be recounted in a review) taken from the author's own pastoral experience. He relates it with perfect taste—a very difficult thing to do under the circumstances—and with profound religious effect. The final chapter, without descending from the high level of value attained by its predecessor, broadens the point of view, giving a swift and true picture of the functions of the Christian Church in modern society.

Oddly enough, just as I am finishing this comment, there comes to me through the mail a clipping from the *New York Times* headed "Plea for Church Unity with Rome issued by 29 High Episcopalians," and containing the assertion that "Protestantism is bankrupt, ethically, culturally, morally, and religiously." One can stand four adverbs ending in "ly" when the manner is so earnest, but one may reflect that only God can know with any certainty whether Protestantism is so utterly insolvent—so quadruply damned. I remember now, what had slipped my mind, that Dr. Hough is a Methodist. And I note that his book exemplifies a kind of catholicity which makes for the reunion of all branches of the Christian Church, culturally and religiously.

§5

THE STORY OF ANGLO-CATHOLICISM

A distinguished example of modern critical history is
Herbert Leslie Stewart's *A Century of Anglo-Catholicism.*[7]
It is at once scholarly and delightful, gravely felt and witty.
The author appreciates the wit that is in other men and has
a fine art of quotation. Above all he has fully realized the
dramatic nature of his subject. This could not be done so
well by a devotee either of modern Catholicism or of modern naturalism. Mr. Stewart is neither. He has the good
fortune (for this purpose) of being "a Presbyterian born
and bred" and professor of philosophy in Dalhousie University in Nova Scotia. From this chair, near but not too
near the stage, he has watched with canny eye the play of
religious life and thought in modern England. And he
shows us that the Anglo-Catholic Movement is a highly
dramatic story—an intensely human "evolution" that rose in
the midst of a century of inhuman evolutionism.

When the thing began in Oxford a hundred years ago
it appeared to the outside world absurdly antiquated in its
ideas and flatly impracticable in its program. The second
point seemed fully proven when "the Oxford Movement"
was deserted by the most gifted of its founders, Newman,
who entered the Roman Catholic Church in 1845. How
many causes have survived, or could survive, such a blow as
this? But the Movement flourished more and more. Today,
says Mr. Stewart, the Anglo-Catholics have practically captured "the machine" of the Church of England. "Most of
the theological colleges are in their hands, so that with them
rests the training of the bulk of the clergy." Their voice is

[7] London and Toronto, 1929.

dominant in ecclesiastic assemblies. They are definitely opposed by only four of the forty-three bishops. Their revision of the Prayer-Book in 1928, though rejected by Parliament, is practically in force. Moreover, their line has gone
forth throughout the earth, though Mr. Stewart does not
say so. He ought to insert a chapter on Anglo-Catholicism
in America and in the mission fields.

His main concern, however, is with Anglo-Catholic
ideas, which so far have been shaped almost entirely in England. His method is to let the champions and opponents of
the Movement speak for themselves in order, adding in each
case his own appraisal. One moment he appears as advocate
and the next as adversary. At times this continual shift of
roles is rendered nonplussing by the author's Scotch habit
of reserving his own deepest convictions. At other times his
insights are somewhat blunted by his prejudices. On the
whole, however, his grasp and his charity are extraordinary.
He helps to realize the hope to which he alludes with characteristic irony in these words: "Religious disputes are notoriously among the most obstinate; and yet, one should not
take for granted that the healing hand of charity must for
ever fail in just that quarter where the praise of charity is
most frequent." As this sentence suggests, Mr. Stewart is
free from the modern error of underestimating the difficulty of true charity. But he sees that honest men "are more
united by their common truthfulness than divided by their
disagreement about what things are true." And his book
demonstrates that real religious charity, as distinguished
from humanitarian emotion, may be advanced by a clear-
cut opposition of differing religious ideas.

He declares he "cannot even faintly share much of the
creed which Anglo-Catholics hold most precious." Yet he
finds that their leaders as a group are the strongest expo-

nents of religious truth today. By tracing Anglo-Catholic ideas through the three chief literary manifestos of the Movement—the *Tracts* of the 1830's, the *Lux Mundi* of 1889, and the *Essays Catholic and Critical* of 1926—he brings out the amazingly quick and rich development of thought that culminates in the last-named volume. As a reader of this volume, I can testify that Mr. Stewart has not overpraised it. Recently England has been comparatively undistinguished in literary and humanistic criticism. But in critical religious thinking she has decisively taken the lead through the work of Von Hügel, the *Essays Catholic and Critical,* and other notable books. With all its faults the volume just mentioned is unrivalled in its combination of the latest scientific knowledge with the best of religious tradition. In other words the Anglo-Catholic Movement has justified itself intellectually as well as practically.

In the practices of the Anglo-Catholic rank and file Mr. Stewart finds and stigmatizes certain dark errors—arrogance, equivocation, ritualistic sentimentality, and superstition verging on idolatry. But his arraignment of modern Protestantism is far more severe. "Casuistry did not cease to be dangerous," he says, "when it became Protestant." Under the pretense of progressiveness, especially in the United States, Protestantism has cringed in countless ways to the fashions of the age and of the world. For one thing, "morality must be smuggled into legislation under the disguise of purposes more attractive than the moral." Protestant casuistry has become deadly for the life of the Kingdom that is not of this world. The Anglo-Catholics are reproached "for turning the Church into an idol" by those who "have turned it rather into a social dodge"!

Mr. Stewart is quite convincing in his argument that the Anglican Church, avoiding the mistake she made regarding

Methodism in the eighteenth century, should do everything in her power to keep the Anglo-Catholics within her fold. As a schismatic body, they would inbreed their errors and eccentricities, and their spiritual and moral power would be much less available for the Christian Church at large. Within the Anglican communion, moreover, they have created "a place for that sort of worshiper not to be classed as either Protestant or Catholic—the sort for whom Romanism is impossible, the old Evangelicalism is absurd, and the new Modernism is no more than an intellectual exercise, but upon whom the historic Faith has none the less laid hold, and for whom the very heart of this is in the symbolism of the Altar." Such persons (including myself) must be especially grateful for this excellent book.

§6

The Pearl of Great Price

By a curious stroke of fate, one of the finest works of art produced by the Anglo-Saxon race was hidden from the public eye for five centuries. The poem called "The Pearl," preserved in a single manuscript in the British Museum, was written about 1370 by an unknown author. His relation to his younger and greater contemporary, Chaucer, resembles that of Spenser (two hundred years afterwards) to Shakespeare. In both cases the elder poet is overshadowed by the large humanity and dramatic power of the younger. But in both cases the elder excels the younger in religious insight and in the art of making the seen and temporal symbolic of the unseen and eternal. Fate was ironic enough, however, to set a quick mark of temporality upon the very language of "The Pearl." The author's native tongue, that of northerly England, was soon displaced in literary usage by the southeastern dialect employed by Chaucer which developed into modern English. Hence "The Pearl"—together with three other poems by the same author, including "Sir Gawain and the Green Knight," the loveliest of the English medieval romances—was tossed aside from the public current of our literature. It remained in manuscript until printed for the Early English Text Society in 1864.

During the past forty years "The Pearl" has attracted much attention from English and American scholars. It has been reissued, in the original or in modern translation, more than a dozen times—but never, until the end of 1932, in such a way as to appeal convincingly to the general reader. This personage may now open side by side two attractive little volumes which will yield him the full treasure of "The Pearl." [8] It is fitting that the fairest text and the most inspired translation of this noble poem should emanate from a college distinguished for its services to belles-lettres—to literature, not primarily as a district for scholastic investigation, but as an art for the delight of every man.

Hitherto the text of the poem has been formidable for all except medieval specialists. But Professor Chase and his eight young colleagues have cleared it of obsolete letters and inserted modern punctuation while retaining the old spelling, which is generally necessary for the subtler qualities of the verse. They employed a facsimile of the manuscript, which has no punctuation and many doubtful passages. Some three hundred of these, with the emendations of previous editors, they have listed in an appendix. Their

[8] *The Pearl* (Bowdoin Edition). The Text of the Fourteenth Century English Poem. Edited by Members of the Chaucer Course in Bowdoin College. Boston, 1932.

The Pearl. Rendered in Modern Verse, with an Introductory Essay, by Stanley Perkins Chase. New York, 1932.

note on the language of the poem should have been more
extensive, I think, and a few more words should have been
included in their excellent glossary. But they have followed
the sound principle, too often and too enragingly neglected
by editors, of not overaiding the reader. For the English
reader the language of "The Pearl," once he gets the swing
of it, is not difficult. It is far from being a rustic dialect. It is
a rich and cultivated speech, first cousin to modern English; narrower than this in range, but superior in a certain
northern brooding plangency that coalesces with the mood
of the poem. Intelligent readers who will grapple in earnest
with the Bowdoin Edition will soon find themselves master-
ing (to quote a line of the text) "the blysful perle with gret
delyt."

But their delight will be swifter and keener if they have
recourse to Mr. Chase's translation. It seems to me to take
its place among the best works of this kind in our language,
quite displacing the previous renditions of the poem. It may
be read entirely for its own sake. But if one reads it alongside the original, stanza for stanza, one sees more and more,
with a catch in the throat and quickened heartbeat, that
here the old and beautiful vision is recaptured: the "Pearl"
is salvaged and reset completely for modern wearing. So
fresh and penetrating is Mr. Chase's insight that it gives
professional English scholars a new understanding of the
poem. Yet his translation is far from being "professional":
it is for Everyman, if I may thus use the title of an old
drama akin to "The Pearl." It is free from the Romantic
grandiloquence mingled with dullness that is apt to char-
acterize the verse of modern college professors. It is the
work of an exact scholar who has also a fine gift in poetry.

Occasionally Mr. Chase uses expressions that are too obsolete, such as "carp" in the sense of "utter." And some-

times he does not reproduce the sinewy impetus of the original. For example, "Love took my joy and left me dearth," is his version of, "I dewyne fordolkëd of luf-daungere," which may be rendered literally: "I pine, sore wounded of love aloof." On the other hand he has managed with rare felicity to reproduce the elaborate rhyme-scheme of the original stanza (ababababbcbc) and the verbal repetitions linking stanza to stanza. And he never misses the tone of visionary graciousness, so to call it, which was so wonderfully conjoined with homely vigor in the very personality (one must believe) of the old nameless poet.

The poet was not a monk, I believe, but a Catholic gentleman who loved the symbols and truths of his religion, looked askance at the dogmatism of contemporary theologians, and kept close to the heart of Everyman. Mr. Chase in the course of his admirable introduction gives a critical summary of the various modern views of the meaning of the poem. He is somewhat too much swayed, I think, by the latest interpretation, that of Sister Madeleva. But he makes clear that the poet's aim was to create, not a logically flawless allegory, but an entrancing episode rich in suggestions of spiritual truth on the one hand and human relationships on the other. The truth on which the poem is based is old and ever new: one must lose one's life to save it. We must lose the objects to which we cling with a too personal devotion—our loved ones, our joys, dogmas, and ideals—in order to find them again in higher form:

> For save the grain in earth lie dead,
> No wheat were won for harvesting.

The action of the poem has three phases (each occupying some thirty-three stanzas) which may be denominated thus:

the lost treasure, the mystery of the queen, the rapture of the King.

In the beginning the narrator is mourning the loss of a priceless pearl which, at some previous time, had slipped from his fingers and rolled down a slope in a lovely garden. Walking now among the luxuriant plants in the height of August, he fancies that they are nourished at root by the dissolved beauty of his pearl. Under the burden of his sorrow and yearning he sinks down upon the flowery hillside. Presently comes a dream-vision, in which the garden is displaced by a region of far nobler beauty—presented to the reader with extraordinary art. Beyond a stream, too deep for crossing, the landscape is still more glorious. Soon the glory centers in the figure of a maiden of pearl-like mien and with yellow hair who appears beneath a cliff beside the water:

> Like gold-thread of embroiderer,
> Her beauty gleamed against that shore,
> While still I looked with mind astir
> Longer, and knew her more and more.

With fear and joy the watcher realizes that this is that which he had lost. The poet with delicate skill suggests that the Pearl may be a lovely child who died in infancy but that, at the same time, she may represent for the reader any good thing that he has loved and lost. The stream, we gather, is the river of death and the girl is in paradise. She speaks. Her tone throughout the ensuing dialogue is strangely fascinating—a free immortal gaiety and a charity void of all false sympathy. She rebukes the poet for the selfishness of his sorrow. He repents and submits to God's laws, and then:

"May bliss attend thee, sir, I pray,"
Said she, her beauty shining clear.
"Be welcome here to walk and stay;
Thy speech now brings me right good cheer."

His thought is now all of her and her celestial life. She wears a crown and he is astonished to learn that she, who was a helpless and ignorant infant on earth, is now a queen of heaven. In reality, her royal state is a symbol of the elevation of the human personality through the death of self. She moves now in a community of souls in which there is no envy or pride, not the slightest sense of inequality even, for God is loved in and through all, and there is no loving of oneself more than one's neighbor. But all this is conveyed through parable and image, particularly the image of the innocent or repurified soul as the bride of Christ. Such souls are royal without taking any precedence of one another, so the maiden tells her listener. At first he is incredulous of this high state of equality. He thinks in terms of earthly rankings, and his deepened humility, fruit of repentance, renders him slow to understand that anything of his (be it his child or his own soul) could really be raised to such a condition. Finally with new awe, gazing upon her and upon the great symbolic pearl that she wears on her breast, he exclaims:

"Unblemished Pearl, in purity
That bear'st," I said, "the pearl of price,
Who formed thy figure? Wise was he
Who wrought thy weeds with craft so nice.
Of Nature's make thou canst not be;
Never Pygmalion's hand precise
Could limn thy face; nor philosophy

> Of Aristotle, thy properties—
>   Thy hue more fair than fleur-de-lys,
>   Thy gracious bearing, Heaven-bred.
>   Tell me, Shining, what virtue is
>   In that thy pearl unblemishëd?"

This is the poet's adoration of the Divine Grace that refashions the human soul, mysteriously, endowing it with queenly beauty.

The talk now turns to the subject of the King in his glory in the New Jerusalem, of which the girl promises the poet a sight. At her direction he ascends a hill on his side of the stream, from which he sees the City of the Apocalypse.

> I stood, dazed as a couching quail,
>   Its strangeness so transported me,
>   Till sense of rest or toil did fail,
>   Or aught but purest ecstasy.

Every descriptive detail in this third and last phase of the poem adds to the steadily mounting rapture of the vision. It culminates in the regal procession of the Lamb and his company through the glorious streets of the City to where "The High God's Self sat on the Throne."

> I scanned His troop; and every mien
>   Life's utter fulness quickenëd.
>   Then saw I there my little queen,
>   Whom I thought near me in the glade.

A mad longing to plunge into the separating stream and make his way to her dissipates the vision. . . . He finds himself again on the hillside in the beautiful garden. Here,

with renewed submission, strength, and peace, he turns to
the high task of making the best of everyday life. In closing, he prays that he and his readers may dedicate themselves anew to that task, both as "homely servants" of God
and as "precious pearls unto His pleasure. Amen. Amen."

That old poem may set us thinking upon all that the following brief parable, preserved in St. Matthew's Gospel
only, has meant for human life and human art: "The kingdom of heaven is like unto a merchant man seeking goodly
pearls: who, when he had found one pearl of great price,
went and sold all that he had, and bought it." Then we may
proceed to recall, one by one, all those things in the human
world that Christ saturated with symbolic meaning. Or
rather, should we not say that He caused them to reveal to
us spiritual values which they always have, and of which,
indeed, they are more or less *composed?* Whenever we
"transvalue" (in a term from current philosophy) an everyday thing, are we not discovering, rather than creating,
some or other quality inherent in it that appears new to us?
Such questions lead to my two last chapters, which are concerned with the symbolic imagination.

9.

A Rumination on the Face

of Nature

§1

JUST NOW I HAVE BEEN LOOKING THROUGH A RECENT SCIEN-
tific book, a precise and exhaustive treatise on *The Evolution of the Human Face from the Face of the Fishes.*
It has amazed and fascinated me. I had not hitherto realized
that "the human face divine" is so fundamentally pisciform.
Often, like any other brooder upon things in general, I had
pondered the affinities between the countenance of man and
the faces of other animals, horse, cow, pig, dog, elephant,
dinosaur, bumblebee, and so on; omitting of course the
monkey, who has become too trite biologically to stir an
up-to-date fancy; but omitting also, and without such justi-
fication, the Face of the Fishes. Here surely an immense
new realm is opened up for the human imagination. There
is much more water than land on the face of the globe, but
so far that face has been confined to *terra firma.* It "stops
with the shore," in Byron's phrase. The shore has promon-
tories like vast human noses, huge teeth of rock gnash the
surge below, and tongues of the land run out; but there
our physiognomy ends. To be sure we speak of the "face
of the deep," but this is a blatantly transferred epithet, thin,
rhetorical. The face of the deep, so far, is an eyeless, fea-
tureless, quite inhuman thing.

The face of the earth, on the other hand, is very intensely human. For it comprises a myriad of animal visages —all the way up from ant to giraffe, including of course the mediocre monkey—which are known to be more or less related to our own. This knowledge comes from poetry, mainly and originally; thence it passes to science to get worked out in detail. Certainly, during the past two centuries, poetry has been extraordinarily aided by science in manifesting our kinship with nature, especially with the animals. But science (in so far as it is not poetry) is interested in rears, not fronts: science from this point of view may be called the back side of poetry. Poetry is concerned with the face of things. At any rate it is poetry that has both caused and *countenanced* the discoveries of natural science. The poetry of modern times has succeeded in revealing in nature a far more intimate and intricate visage than was known to men of old. It has humanized the face of the earth in innumerable ways.

Walt Whitman, for example, put a fresh meaning into the faces of cows. Certain ancient religious cults made the cow divine; Whitman made her human. In those old cults she symbolized the divine fertility of nature; in Whitman she represents the fertile idleness of man—that large, cud-chewing vacancy which every industrious citizen ought to enjoy occasionally, and from which he may return to his work with new sapotaceous energy. That idle mood is most at home in sunny prairies and meadows; where we may recall, cheerfully, the fact that all flesh is grass, notably the flesh of cows, and roast beef merely grass well done; and where, herbivorous in our very souls but eschewing all herbs of toxic working, such as De Quincey's poppy or the lotus of young Tennyson, we are content, for the time being,

In the undulating fields to live and lie reclined
On the grass, with cows together, careless of mankind.

Whitman, of course, went further. For if man, generally speaking, is a religious animal, such, peculiarly speaking, was the case of Walt Whitman. And so while humanizing the cow he did not make her less divine; he touched her with solemn thought. He did not exactly revive the archaic bovine divinity, but he summoned us to venerate in nature and in man a sort of divine bovinity. No doubt he deified his own rare zest for ruminant relaxation. This fact must be admitted from the standpoint of cold criticism; but I happen to be cold to that standpoint just at the present moment. For out there beyond my windows in a summer retreat in New England the meadows, rolling between the Atlantic Ocean and me, are gay with sun and wind. The tall brown and green grasses are interspersed with purple vetch and white marguerites—and with Dutch Belted cows, very worthy creatures, scenically and gastronomically.

Suddenly I recall a famous local episode bearing upon the religion of bovinity. Some years ago, on All Hallows' Eve, a band of undergraduates belonging to a venerable college in a near-by town led a cow up the winding staircase of their collegiate chapel and deposited her in the belfry, whence she was removed with great difficulty by a gang of workmen in the dawn of All Hallows' Day. Significantly the sacred beast went up more easily than she came down. Doubtless those pious students were not fully aware of the significance of their rite. They were not trying to discredit the Congregational Faith that had nurseled the infancy of their college. That faith to be sure was less vital to them than it had been to their forebears; but they were not demanding that it be overtopped by the ancient exaltation of the cow. However, many great pranks in the drama of human history have been symbolical far beyond the intention of the actors. And it is a fact that scores of hoarier creeds than Congregationalism have been outlasted by the antique veneration of the cow; which still obtains in India and is engaged in by one of the leading intellectuals of our time, Mr. Gandhi; who is known to be much influenced by the Occidental nature poets, including Walt Whitman.

Many cults shall pass away but the cult of the cow shall not pass away—not till human civility disappears from the face of the earth. At the present time more and more critics are urging that modern civilization, like that of Greece and Rome, may be weakened fatally by excessive urbanization. Fully conscious of this danger I would point out that one sign of it is the attitude of the modern civilian towards the cow. At best he views her idyllically: when he ascends the hills in vacation time he likes to see herds of cows, if not hordes of golfers, dotting the outspread landscape. Mainly, however, he regards her as at once a practical necessity and a practical joke. Now certainly the cow has those three aspects: she is idyllic, beefy-milky, and often quite absurd. But also she is the perennial symbol—not a *mere* but a *real* symbol, an inherent feature, an organic outgrowth—of the mystic, vast, leisurely, benign fertility of nature. And I claim that, whatever practical measures may be taken to fill up the modern breach between the town and the farm, this division will never be healed *in spirit* till the industrious citizen, including the commercialized farmer, relearns the religious meaning of the word bovinity. A catholic civility, embracing and uniting the life of the city and the life of the country, must comprise a due and right veneration for the Cow.

Far be it from me to urge that the cow should become

a prominent object on the premises of the modern church. The seductive example cited above should not, I believe, be followed literally; cows ought not to be placed in our belfries: the cow bell and the church bell must be kept on different levels. Nor should cows be installed in the pulpits or side chapels or other sacred recesses of Protestant and Catholic edifices. Perhaps the life-size effigy of a small and good-looking calf—marble, of course, not gold—might be placed in a sunlit nook near the church's south entrance. But bearing in mind the difficulty which organized religion has continually had, before and since the time of Moses, in keeping within bounds the veneration of sacred images, I admit that even a white replica of the super-innocent calf (cows are innocent and therefore calves are super-innocent) might be a source of embarrassment on ecclesiastical grounds. To be sure, certain highly enlightened congregations, urban and crowded with culture, belonging mayhap to the Unitarian or Christian-Scientific communions, might well adopt my suggestion without any damage and perhaps with spiritual profit. But I do not insist upon the point. However, I do insist that, if the cow is not to come into the church, the church should go out to the cow. In other words the modern church should push out into the countryside in a very vigorous manner, opening herself to its influence as well as bringing her own to bear upon it.

§ 2

In early days in Europe pagan temples and afterwards Christian temples, particularly monastic churches, were erected in more or less open places—in localities which, at least when compared with the modern city, were scantily inhabited. And there today, with the thin surrounding population thinned away into air, many of them are still to be seen, in ruins, in tilted blocks and thick pillars and fine shafts, in round and pointed arches; utterly opened to Nature now; while modern churches in nearby cities are increasingly shut away from her, packed into populations that every day grow denser. . . . On a certain evening some years ago, after visiting the ruins of a monastic cathedral in a lovely open countryside not far from London, I happened to dine with the rector of a church that stood jammed amidst the shops, warehouses, and tenements of a slummy square near the center of the city. "I have to keep fighting for my lights," he declared, in a phrase that was unintentionally but significantly ambiguous. I knew that he was battling against heavy odds to establish his Christian message in the souls of that dingy neighborhood; but he meant that only through bellicose vigilance was he able to prevent new walls of "the Wen," as Cobbett called London, from cutting off entirely the sparse rays of light that managed to enter the windows of his church. I thought of the sunlight flooding the beautiful, roofless, meadow-girt ruin not many miles away.

Decadent or weak in the country and with her "lights" often dimmed in the city, the church has erred from nature along with industrial civilization. To be sure, the church— by which I mean organized and official religion of all kinds and in all times—was in early days far too pagan, that is, too rural, or, at worst, too naturalized. In the pagan cities of the Roman Empire the "church," no longer vitally rustic, was falsely naturalized. Hence when Christianity gained control of her, it was natural for her to aspire intensely above nature and, in some degree, away from nature. And it was natural in the later Middle Ages for the new commercial town to cluster below the cathedral spire, as com-

merce should center in religion. But to cluster around a
church is one thing, to swamp it with civic construction is
another. Owing to the industrial revolution and to the sins
of the Church herself, she is now deluged with urbanity.
In their recognition of that bad fact, our advanced religionists, those who advocate "nature," are right; but their ways
of remedying it are wrong. They themselves are fatally ur-
banized and one sees that they are reacting violently from
themselves. The spectacle of ministers in pulpits shut off
from the country by several square miles of stores, banks,
factories, and residences, preaching that religion should be
natural, is a very unnatural spectacle. The naturalistic doctrines that these men adore recall the hopeless nature-gods
of the sophisticated cities of the Roman Empire.

The true pagan health that belongs to the life of the
Church can be recovered and developed only when she
lives and works and thinks as fully in the country as in the
city. Nor otherwise can modern society be cured of its
urban heart disease; for where society worships, worships
corporately, there in the long run will its heart be also.
Certainly the Church must maintain her civic altars together with that urbane reason, slow result of the ages,
which, under the Grace of God, freed her from the primitive yoke of nature, and enabled her eventually to comprise
the physical universe in catholic religious philosophy; notably that of St. Thomas Aquinas. But in the thirteenth century nature had not yet been dissected and mechanized by
that civilian science and industry which the Church did so
much to foster; the country was still far from being out-
weighed by the city. The angelic philosopher came at a
happy moment for a true vista of nature. Aquinas, incidentally, knew the country before he knew the city; whereas
many religious thinkers today know Aquinas before they

know the country, if they know. Aquinas at all. Many of
them believe that he has been rendered obsolete by modern
civic naturalism. . . . The modern revival of rural monasti-
cism, inside and outside of the Roman Catholic Church, can
do much to restore the pagan health of religion (I am using
the word "pagan," of course, in its etymological sense) if
the monks become and remain, as they failed to do of yore,
real farmers and herdsmen, material and spiritual shepherds.
But the problem is far wider than that and it ought to engage the attention of all branches of the Church, especially
in the United States.

§3

In the early nineteenth century it could still seem likely
that America was destined to readjust the face of the earth
by balancing the overgrowing old-world cities with her
vast open spaces. These allured the discontented imagina-
tions of Europe. Chateaubriand came to our wilds to in-
dulge his questionable nature worship. Byron did not come
but sent his oratorical fancy diving

> Deep in the unpruned forest, 'midst the roar
> Of cataracts, where nursing Nature smiled
> On Infant Washington. . . .

And it was natural and reasonable that Jefferson and others
should envisage the future United States as a great federation of agricultural communities. Such an America would
indeed have counterpoised citified Europe and made the
look of the globe more natural again. But ironically enough
our great woods and open spaces, by opening the American
mind and making it very impressible, and by stimulating its

practical and pioneering faculty while offering untold stores of the raw materials of industry, opened us wide to the influence of European industrialism and lured us to carry this to an extraordinary extreme.

So it appears that our mighty wilds, once adored by Europeans, have promoted a phenomenon now deplored by Europeans—the Americanization of Europe. However, the original sin, which those mourners should mainly bewail, was the Europeanizing of America. She is giving back to Europe that which Europe taught her but she has bettered the instruction. The two grand discoveries made by modern Europe, the continent of America and the religion of material success, might have served providentially to counteract each other. No doubt those two achievements were congenitally related but certainly they were not foredoomed to coalesce entirely. They were first cousins, let's say, at birth; but through a series of rebirths due to occidental "progress" they have now become Siamese twins. That morbid bond is ripe for cutting, and American surgery is called for. Many of our citizens are fired with a desire to help mankind at large in ways which seem more kindly than that sharp operation. But surely in the long run America may best serve the world by severe efforts at home, efforts inevitably long and painful, to dissolve her unnatural ties with the cult of factory-progress and to sculpture out her own true character.

Accordingly the popular cry for a "hundred-per-cent Americanism" ought to be refined and directed, rather than ridiculed, by our American intellectuals, whose ideas on the whole are abnormally exotic though their country has now an abnormal need of indigenous thinking. Such thinking can be as open to the inpour of foreign ideas as the soil is to the rain, but it must transform them entirely, as the

growths of the soil transform the rain, through constant
native working. Our traditional foreign policy of avoiding
foreign entanglements should appear as the historic symbol
of a new endeavor to solve our domestic tangle, our feverish
urban muddle foreign to the nature of the land. The land
has been so foreignized by the quick inrush of the nations
that an exceptional detachment is the right course now for
America so long as it means, not a formal and sterile isolation, but a vital process of isolating (in the chemical sense
of the word) the land's true personality. America, discovered from without, must be rediscovered from within; settled from across the seas, she must be resettled by Americans. And any attempts on her part at improving the
world's features will always seem somewhat unnatural until
she succeeds in finding her own natural aspect.

The skyscraper, regarded in Europe as the symbol of
America, should be regarded in America as a late symbol
of Europe, as on offshoot and upshoot of the European
lust of size and power in a land where new towns afforded
sites and the earth sufficient iron ore. The thing is absurdly
anomalous on the surface of this wide country, which ab-
sorbs and belittles it to next to nothing. It is no more outstanding than a needle stuck in an acre, for a truly American vision. But for European eyes (on either side of the
ocean) the needle blots out the landscape, looming up as
the spire of the latest European religion; gazed at with
pious horror; dominating the whole of the American skyline as fully as it does the skyline of New York—a city
which, because it stands for Europe in America, is America
in the eyes of Europe. The soul of the skyscraper was en-
gendered in London, mainly, but its body could not be
born there: the skyline was preoccupied with the steeples
and domes of an older religion; and the dubious soil be-

neath, threatening to give way under St. Paul's Cathedral, could not sustain the additional load of the Empire State Building. This had to take bodily form in New York; where, by a geologic accident full of religious meaning, the ground was a long, narrow rock inviting long-up, narrow buildings.

That rock, of course, was not counted on by our early European settlers. On the contrary many of them had in their hearts the deep cry of the Psalmist: "God is the rock of my heart, and my portion forever." But in the hearts of their successors "God" was changed to "New York." Historians have recently shown how the energeia of Protestantism produced the modern gospel of material work and profit, notably in America. Thus a peripheral speck of the new gigantic continent, a tiny bucktooth of rock, an insignificant jut from the face of the plains and mountains was transformed by religious magic into the civil promontory now known as New York. Unlike old York, or old Amsterdam, which, however commercialized during the modern era, are nevertheless deep-rooted in the countries to which they belong, this new city is a radical distortion of the land. It is a natural projection, not of the American continent, but of the religion of our early European immigrants. The New Jerusalem they came to build eventuated in New York. Like this city, the profile of their faith was hard, narrow, and lofty; the spires and domes of elder cults were overtopped by its skyline. At its best it was noble. Its bleakness has been exaggerated by up-to-date Americans who do not see how much bleaker is its modern offspring, the cultus of Manhattan. The faithful for whom the life of New York is just the reverse of bleak should try to grasp the fact that such was the case of Puritanism for the faithful. In fact, the deceased village of Boston, if studied and

revived by regardful imagination, appears fertile and warm
alongside New York City. But alongside America, the true
face of America, they both look bleak and meagre. American civilization was erected by a faith far too narrow for
the land.

§4

That fact, no doubt, is more or less true of every civilization; but ours is the extreme example. The older civilizations, including the European, the youngest of them all,
expanded their narrow beginnings in a manner closely related to the deliberation of Nature. The prehistoric Asiatics
who gradually discovered Europe, permeating forests and
reaching coast lines novel and vast to them, adapted their
ancient cults to the nature of the new continent in a vitally
gradual manner. They developed their religion slowly as
they slowly developed the face of the land. At length they
were ready for Christianity when, following them from
Asia, it overcame and fed upon rites and philosophies akin
to it in spirit. Thus through long centuries, twelve after
Christ and as many and more before Him, the Eurasians
built a religion catholic enough for Europe. Conceivably
a similar development could have taken place in America—
if those Asiatics who chose to cross the Bering isthmus
long ago, becoming the Amerindians, had been followed
by other and ever deeper waves of immigration reaching
back as far as Mediterranean shores; if early Europe and
Christianity had come to America through slow Asia. But
the sea cut America from Asia, and man cut Asia from Europe, thwarting thus a natural eastward circulation of Eurasian culture. America, left primitive, was a powerful hidden
conductor to which eventually the pent-up energy of Eu-

rope suddenly flashed over. The civilizing of America, seen against the background of the aeons of Eurasian growth, is an amazing short circuit. Here the process of civilization, hitherto a slow tide, becomes an electric current; swift and thrilling enough and mighty in its way, but too mechanic and straitened.

Certainly that particular jet of old-world energy which, after making the unprecedented and exhilarating leap to the New World, could there overtop all other forces whether old or new, had to be extremely powerful and correspondingly narrow. It had to be a tense concentration of the culture of Europe in one special direction. It had to be something like what it actually was, or became—Industrious Protestantism. But this great cult was better fitted for rapidly exploiting the resources of a new soil than for the full discovery of the spirit of a new country. No doubt the intense supernatural light that Puritanism threw upon our stony northeast coast was a beginning of the revealing of a higher self for America. But to incarnate that self in the very flesh of the land, to cultivate the supernatural life in and through the natural life, to maintain the height of the Christian faith while rebuilding the Church in vital correspondence with the vast and complex face of the new land and nation—that task was far too large for Industrious Protestantism. That cult could cover, but could not discover, America.

Europe discovered America as the lightning discovers an oak, and America has not yet succeeded in recovering from that discovery. Her natural growth has proceeded only in a maimed fashion while she has provided handy and abundant timber for the rehousing of old-world cults. So far she is the land of sects, of extreme creeds and extreme reactions, and of narrow attempts at being broad-minded. For her civil history coincides with the violent sectionalizing of the European mind. Europe in the Middle Ages broadened and solidified in the finding of herself; then split into strenuous cults, religious, tribal, economic, in the finding of America. Ancient Europe absorbed St. Paul and went on to St. Thomas Aquinas with his wide and sound grasp of nature in relation to supernature. But presently the Pauline theories re-erupted in a form prodigiously unnatural in the work of John Calvin, and overflowed to America. Europe, though badly shaken by the Calvinistic spirit (in the most inclusive sense of this term), could in time digest the portent because of her catholic training. She could make the grass grow pretty well over the Calvinistic lava. Not so America, in spite of her great prairies. She was Calvinized, and galvanized, into civilization; and her mind still suffers badly from Calvinistic galvanism.

In other words, this America, this grand new front of nature, was occupied most determinedly by men who were determinedly reacting from nature. This vast and fecund section of the Earth's temperate zone—which, unlike the rest of that zone, had missed its natural period of pagan civilization—called for a Christianity with plenty of pagan blood in its veins and a pagan breadth of imagination; instead of a Christianity that was trying to extrude from its spirit and its forms every last pagan element. The dark religious gulf between the early and the late Eurasian settlers in America—that is, between the Indians and the New Englanders—signifies a dark hiatus in natural American history. And the treatment accorded the natives in the past three centuries by us newcomers is indicative of our treatment, so extremely brash and fickle, of American nature in general, nature physical and spiritual. We have exploited and wasted her and sentimentalized over her, pummelled her

piously and indulged her violently, veneered and venereal-
ized her. By now we have done about everything to her
except understand and control her with native religious
capacity. We shall not come to right terms with her, mentally and esthetically, morally and economically, until we
achieve a scope of religious thought and technique comparable to that attained by Europe in the height of the Middle Ages—and yet, truly American.

§5

We Americans must never cease to hear the clarion call
of Emerson for a fresh, large spirituality to match and comprehend the breadth of nature in America. But we have to
leave behind his blindness to the fact that the consummation he so devoutly wished is impossible without the Church
—without socially organic and organized religion. While
Emerson as a young man was breaking with the Church
and deciding that religion was "not now tending to a cult,"
a powerful cult called the Oxford Movement was incubat-
ing in England; and in many other ways Christianity was
preparing to renew her depleted institutional life. But the
greatest of American writers had a great suspicion of religious institutionalism, partly because he was an American,
partly because he was Emerson. Moreover, a certain thriv-
ing cult to which he unwittingly belonged had as one of its
mainsprings—with fundamental irony—a strong aversion to
cults.

The cult of ideal individualism that rose in the seventeenth century, flowered in the eighteenth, fruited in the
nineteenth, and rotted in the twentieth, is responsible for
the dream that religion can flourish without the Church;
citizenship without the Nation; art without the Art Tradi-

tion; and knowledge without the College, i.e., that the most reliable insight into the meaning of life is obtained by a sort of intuition hostile to organized intellectual effort. Such was the hasty and vivid dream. But the very latest findings of sociological anthropology, confirmed by the latest events on the stage of human history, remind us of the fact that from first to last man is an institutional animal. To conceive of "man and nature" over against institutions is to make an abstraction from nature; institutions are nature. When man makes a strenuous effort to be more natural, he alters his institutions, for better or for worse. When he alters them for the better he becomes more highly natural.

It is unnatural to try to be natural by being non-institutional, and the self-reliance thus acquired is distinctly unreliable. Human personality results from human institutions and can grow above them only in proportion as it is deeply rooted in them. To rise above institutional life, in a real instead of illusory fashion, is to be as much a part of it as a tree is of the land. This is a true enough image for the life of a great man; and it serves to correct the hyperboles of Romantic individualism in regard to the nature of genius. Carlyle, for instance, preached that "the Hero is a free force direct from God's own hand." But this doctrine, true of the Holy Ghost, is not true of human persons however great they may be. It emblemizes a spiritual truth, but it is not that historical truth which Carlyle, by confusing two realms of thought, deemed it to be. While rejecting metaphysics in favor of the historical method he maintained a metaphysical view of the great men of history. He conceived them as precreated and thrust into the human drama in a catastrophic fashion, which his amazing imagination strove to picture as natural, or, to adopt his own phrase, as supernaturally natural; weaving across the rift in his thought a tense and many-colored web of persons and events. But great men become unbelievable and history, which Carlyle proclaimed a divine revelation, appears an insubstantial pageant unless great men and history are seen to be correlative; unless Heroes are created in and through human institutions; unless history makes great men as much as they make history.

Carlyle loved history not wisely but too well; his violent embrace of it was like to strangle its meaning, and certainly helped to do so for his chief friend in America. Emerson in any case loved history not at all and thought we Americans would do well to leave it behind us. And indeed in his time the story of America could easily seem unique enough to disqualify history—and heroic enough to disqualify the uniqueness of Heroes. Therefore Carlyle's laudation of great men was transferred by Emerson to the human spirit in general, much to Carlyle's dismay. The aristocratic thunders uttered by the older prophet, the Elijah of Craigenputtock, were followed hard upon by the democratic lightnings, so serenely violent, of the Elisha dwelling in Concord. Carlyle confused Time and Eternity, history and metaphysics, in favor of great men. Emerson did so on behalf of general human nature. In a way Emerson's vision was deeper than his friend's. If Carlyle gave to Heroes what was due to the Holy Ghost, Emerson certainly endeavored to give the Holy Ghost his due; but unfortunately he was apt to confuse the Holy Spirit with the human spirit in general. The "Soul," his favorite entity, is not the simple unity that his unitarian genius conceived it to be. Emerson's "Soul" is a flexible combination of God, man, nature, and Emerson, lofty and pure in purport but yet an unholy mixture unless holily employed. Emerson so employed it. But America, including Walt Whitman, Emerson's most vivid disciple, happens to be, on a rough calculation, ninety per cent unholy.

Emerson's religious book on *Nature*, written just a hundred years ago, his first important work and containing in embryo all the rest, is a new and great chapter of Occidental scripture. In form it is a loose, ebullient sketch, but the outline it gives to its subject is grander than that attained by the writer's master, Wordsworth, or by any of the other leading Romantic naturists. They surpassed Emerson in the architecture of verse and prose, but could not equal him in the noble comprehensiveness of his treatment of nature, ranging from critical shrewdness to high mystical insight. But although comparatively catholic in its vision of nature, the book is quite uncatholic in the nature of its religion. Institutional religion is lightly daffed aside while nature is erected into a religious institution. The Introduction summons Americans away from religious tradition; but the final chapter summons George Herbert, the Anglican cleric of the seventeenth century, to testify on behalf of the religious tradition of nature—Herbert, whose nature poetry is a fine flower on the tree of Catholic Christianity. Also, the prophetic power of Emerson himself was nourished under the surface, as his writings frequently hint, by the roots of that same tree. Nature could be a great church for him because a great church had embraced nature.

Certainly Emerson's prophecy can come true. Certainly in new America, as in old Europe and Asia, nature can become a religious institution; but not without the aid of institutional religion. Perhaps there has never been such a great and spiritual person who was at the same time so unsympathetic as Emerson to the constant human necessity of historical religion. Throughout his long life Emerson was dazzled by the brilliant discovery, made when he was

a young pastor—and hard, as a rule, for young pastors to
make at that time in New England—the discovery of the
remarkable discrepancy between organic religion and organic nature in the land in which he found himself. He
could admire at a distance the catholic forms of the Christian faith. In a passage of his diary, written a dozen years
after his religious book on *Nature*, he declares that the
Catholic Church is superior to Protestantism because of
being "in harmony with Nature" (*Journals*, October 18,
1847). But he found no church, and conceived of none,
equal to the great America expanding before his eyes. He
reacted extremely from the narrow church of his ancestors.
In doing so, however, he carried on its narrowness in a
changed fashion. Its straitness of creed became in him a
straitness of imagination. In trying to expand and naturalize
the Puritan theology he lost what scope the Puritans had
of religious imagination. Puritanism, a great church in its
way, a vital branch of the Christian Communion, had a
vivid apprehension of that historic and social corpus which,
whatever else it may be, is the most broadly human of all
religious symbols. But Emerson restricted his religious symbols, unnaturally, to nature. His most spiritual paragraphs,
if read alongside passages from the chief Puritan divines,
appear inhumanly meagre in their imaginative cast—except
in the eyes of readers whose religious instincts have been
desiccated by Emersonian individualism.

This, in one form or another, became the prevalent credo
of the American mind, while the American heart was going in for the much more dramatic religion of industrial
achievement. New York took our fancy while Boston kept
hold of our mind. As the railways pushed inland in the
middle of the past century, Emerson extended his lecture
tours farther and farther westward. Boston, so to speak,

was making a valiant effort to spiritualize our locomotion
and, at the same time, to expand her own religious mind in
response to the new national life. But the task was too
large and difficult for the time, and for Boston. She did indeed extend and quicken her spiritual "intellection" (Emerson's significant word) but only by attenuating a far more
vital function of the mind, the religious imagination. And
now the other and vivider cult, the religion of mass production, is also losing its hold on our imagination. Two tall
spires, each handsome in its way, are retreating to our rear
horizon—the steel skyscraper of New York and the spiritual one of Boston. Each has now an air of static aspiration.
And both of these cults go back to the fact that American
civility, built up with unnatural speed, was originated by
a species of European Christianity far too narrow for the
land.

<h2 style="text-align:center">§6</h2>

American religion, if it is to become catholic enough for
America, must learn a great deal from nature on the one
hand and, on the other, from the Middle Ages. Those two
ways of learning, so far from being incompatible, are complementary to each other; they can aid and correct each
other. Religion when truly catholic is never divorced from
nature but always hostile to theories that confuse nature and
deity. Such theories are opposed by nature itself when nature is plainly and normally known. They are the perennial
product of partial views of nature combined with attenu-
ated, and often disguised, religious emotion. Modern naturism, emanating from the studios, parlors, and parks of
European or Europeanized society, is foreign to the native
genius of America. It has no roots, excepting those created
by sentimental fancy, in the American soil. Walt Whitman

as a nature priest was a European lounger in America; hence his intense appeal to European studios. His variety of religion was no more truly American than that of the deistic Indian of Pope's *Essay on Man*. The actual religion of our Indians, as recent scholars have more and more shown, was normally theistic, and sometimes nobly so; and the same was the case of our frontiersmen. Pantheistic naturism is the product of the studio. Practical and vital contact with nature fosters the conception of God that characterizes catholic religion.

To encourage that kind of contact with nature should surely be a main concern of the Church, of organized religion in all its branches, particularly in America. Just now our Catholics, Protestants, and Jews are undertaking a strong crusade against the immoral moving picture. But this evil is merely one of the surface results, albeit the most picturesque, of the immoral urbanization of American society. The American moving picture is so often immoral because the American countryside has become for most of our citizens nothing but a moving picture. They dash across it hither and thither in vehicles of ever increasing speed on paved ways or through the air; or, seated in the movie palace, they watch it "jittering" across the screen. Its grandeur and repose escape them except in sentimental moments which do not affect their lives. America, just five centuries ago a quiet and slow quarter of the world, devoid even of horses, is now the world's chief symbol of noise and crowd and speed. And this disorder has heavily infected American religion. Therefore the numerous church-goers who are now (so it is reported) boycotting moving pictures should employ the leisure, thus attained, in contemplating critically the moving-picture spirit that there is in our churches. That spirit is of the city, the abnormal American city; and the Church can effectually counteract it only when she sets herself to live and work and think in vital contact with the soil.

The particular measures necessary to bring about that end can be determined only by our religious leaders. Any suggestions offered by a mere literary onlooker, especially by one enjoying a summer vacation, would be likely to appear somewhat trivial or visionary. Two projects, however, insist on coming to my mind. I should like to call them practical; but as I contemplate them I feel myself relapsing towards that mood of comparative levity in which this rumination began.

First I would urge that no more cathedrals or other great religious structures should be erected in our cities. Every citizen asked to contribute to a grand new church or synagogue should stipulate that it be placed at least ten miles from the nearest town in the midst of a hundred acres of grounds, with adequate provision for the transport of carless worshipers. Of course the design of the edifice would harmonize with the countryside; the architect would be encouraged to imitate nature afresh, forgetting the factory lines that have of late been creeping into ecclesiastic architecture. This project would open a clear channel for the vast religious energies which we Americans have devoted to programs that have proved to be far less practicable, such as World Peace and Prohibition. Thus the United States would gradually become dotted with noble rural temples—living successors to the ruined ones that our tourists admire on old-world landscapes; successors, too, of those vanished shrines all over the wild face of the land where the Great Spirit, and lesser spirits, were worshiped by congregations of the aboriginal American Church, that of the Indians.

My second and more important suggestion is that our religious workers should engage so far as possible in the working of the soil. Emerson tried to be a farmer and lamented that he was an ill one. More lamentable is the fact that his ecclesiastic successors, our advanced and gifted preachers who are trying to naturalize religion, are not farmers at all. They speak from pulpits embedded in acres of concrete, stone, and steel. Their contact with nature, outside of cities and books, is that of summer vacations. Now, a summer vacation is a natural and proper thing for men of letters who believe in ecclesiastic tradition, but not for ecclesiastics who disdain that tradition and believe mainly in nature. Vacational contemplation of nature, even when accompanied by ardent golf and boating, can give us only the surfaces and the sentiment of nature. The true foundation of natural religion has always been and will always be plain economic toil in forest and in field, closely interfused with the spirit of meditation and worship. Nowadays when that toil and that spirit are so widely sundered, surely the sort of minister to whom I am referring should be the first of all to throw himself into the breach. The saintliest of their number should immolate themselves on the altar of this cause by getting themselves transferred from urban to rustic parishes. All of them, disdaining the traditional summer vacation as ardently as they disdain the traditional dogmas of the Church, should purchase modest farms—ploughland, pasture, woodlot—and resort thither for labor on every possible occasion. They should become familiar with spade, axe, and hoe, and their bottoms should know the seats of harrows, reapers, and milking stools.

If this great example were set by our naturistic preachers it would have an immense effect upon the Church in general. The cry "Back to the soil!" would loudly resound from the throats of bishops, priests, rabbis, deacons, and other ministers—including, I trust, the leaders of Buchmanism or the Oxford Group Movement, the most striking religious cult in America at the present moment. The good results it has achieved can render a brooding onlooker tolerant of its strident ways, its public confessions and "go-getting" conversions. Organic religion, after all, must use contemporary organs; and lurid advertising is better employed in saving our souls than in making us spend more money on the cigarettes that perish. Fire must often be fought with fire. But in this case the scene will presently be mere ashes unless great care is taken to foster the growth of slow, living things in the wake of the rapid fire. And as a matter of historic fact every religious movement that has been sufficiently inspired and enlightened by the authentic flame has presently found methods of counteracting its own extremes. Early Christianity produced a wild speaking with tongues, but soon it produced a St. Paul to articulate and steady that first fine careless rapture—notably in the free and wayward western outpost of Corinth. Westward the course of loud-speaking, apparently, takes its way. Well, the leaders of our Buchmanism, by way of counteracting its exhausting noisiness without chilling the warm truth of its spirit, should try to induce many of its converts to devote themselves to a period of laconic labor on farms. Some of these persons would no doubt develop into permanent rural saints, influencing the population more by example than by speech. What America needs today is agricultural hermits. And we shall be sure that Buchmanism is an integral, saving part of our American life as soon as we see many Buchmanites silently milking cows.

§7

The Cow, the Church, the United States—a thoughtless reader might complain that these are queer topics for a rumination on nature. But a prophetic reader will perceive that those three natural institutions are bound to bulk large in the period just ahead of us. They are the three main aspects that the riddling visage of the old Sphinx wears for us at present. Man's endless task and adventure in the unfolding of nature will go awry in the twentieth century unless he attends wisely to those three features of nature. What meaning have they in common? What will America do to the Church and to the Cow, and what will they do to America? Our fate hangs on the answer. The trend of modern society in all parts of the globe will be very largely determined by the extent to which we find the right interrelation of those three institutions, America, Church, and Cow.

"For Earth, that gives the milk, the spirit gives. . . ." So sang George Meredith, the last (he was nine years younger than Whitman) of the chief modern nature poets. Like the others he was so intoxicate of the new "milk" he was drawing from Earth that he found it easy to fancy that the "spirit"—all of it, not just some of it—came from Earth too. That was a natural error for a vigorous poet who was reacting from the Church. A lusty infant whose mother's breasts have proved to be inadequate for him, and whose growth is therefore ministered to by a Guernsey in the neighborhood, would exclaim, if he could think like Meredith, "The cow, that gives the milk, the spirit gives"—nature, who mothers my lustihood, is the mother of my soul. However, as a matter of fact, the Christian Church, rather than nature, is the mother of modern nature poetry. But at the time when she was suckling it her health was decidedly below par; she was weak with schism and dry with controversy. In the twelfth century she had been able to absorb and Christianize the earthy muse of the troubadours. But in the eighteenth century she could not retain in her embrace the modern interest in nature which she had initially inspired. Therefore the new poets more and more transferred "the spirit" from Christianity over into the realm of nature, mixing it with "the milk." And as late as the time of Meredith—but no later, I think—an excellent, mature, and comprehensive mind could still deem modern naturism more catholic in its outlook than the genius of Christianity. Meredith in 1880 could write sincerely and solemnly the line I have quoted above; *no Meredith* could do so today.

Emerson could chant in his Concord: "Over me soars the eternal sky, full of light and of deity. . . ." "Of cosmic rays and of theory," we should have to write it today. Today natural science, more competent than ever in the realm of investigation, has become fatally crude and confused in its metaphysical notions. The same condition appears on the practical plane in our economic confusion. Our immense material progress during the past three centuries has merely intensified the problem that Shakespeare saw three centuries ago: "Distribution should undo excess and each man have enough." Our immense accumulation of scientific knowledge has brought about at the same time a revival of the primitive metaphysical notions of pre-Socratic Greece. Windy heads and empty bellies—these are the natural results of an amazing scientific and economic grasp of nature attained on the merely natural level. Surely the modern age has thoroughly demonstrated the fact that nature cannot be truly understood and utilized apart from the supernatural, and that the supernatural cannot be socially real without the agency of the Church. Apart from the organized social effort at apprehending God, man in society loses the way of comprehending nature. The beautiful words of Emerson, cited above, recalling as they do the sublimer words of the Nineteenth Psalm, are at once reminiscent of and prophetic of the Temple.

At the present time nature poetry, the index of our total attitude to nature, is in a state of exhaustion from which it cannot firmly recover until the idea of nature is again dominated by the idea of the Temple. When organic religion has regained its normal hold on the poetic imagination, this in turn will exert a beneficent influence on natural science and economics. In the meanwhile, however, what are our poets to do, those many who are still swayed by the pantheistic or atheistic view of nature coming down from the eighteenth century? We cannot wish them to be idle while perforce awaiting a religious "New Deal." And it seems to me clear, on the face of things, just what they should do:

"I saw a new heaven and a new earth," exclaimed St. John the Divine, or another man with the same name; then he added lucklessly, being a devoted landsman, "and there was no more sea." This was clearly an error in the Christian revelation according to St. John. Out there beyond the meadows of my summer retreat in New England, beyond the swaying grasses and the Dutch Belted cows, the tide of the ocean is rising, swinging up a great bay. And here on the desk at my elbow is the book that started my rumination, *The Evolution of the Human Face from the Face of the Fishes*. The modern nature poet has now exhausted the land but has hardly done more than begin on the sea. He has plunged deep in the soil, latterly in the mud; he should now plunge deep in the ocean. Having wonderfully humanized the face of all the earth, he should now do the same for the sea and all that therein is. We human beings have long been accustomed to noting particular piscine features in members of our species, as "a fishy eye," "a fishlike mouth." But the heights and depths of Piscine Nature have not been explored by poetry. A century ago certain poets looked with new reverence upon the grazing ass, but they entirely neglected the grazing lobster. Whitman loved the cow but overlooked the sea cow. He was inspired by our bovinity. It is high time for his successors to adore our pisciformity. In short, while the Church goes out to the country, as I have urged above, our nature poets should go out to sea. Later the Church can take the sea in too. She can rescue it from wrong naturalism when she has rescued the land. One thing at a time seems to be the law for spirits at work on the face of nature.

A conservative Catholic critic who read the ensuing final chapter in manuscript remarked to me that, in his opinion, it was subtly unorthodox. He meant, though he was too courteous to use just these words, that it was a misleading thing, moving dubiously in the outskirts of Christianity. As for my treatment of the altar, he declared that the least important fact regarding the Christian altar is that it is a symbol. But my point, as I hope the reader will see, is that the most important fact regarding a symbol is that it may be an altar. However, I think that we may regard the Christian altar as *entirely* a symbol if we are orthodox, i.e., right and sound (even if we are also modern), in our view of what a symbol *entirely* is.

10.

A Reflection on the Nature of Symbols

VISIBLE SYMBOLS ARE OBVIOUSLY OF THREE KINDS: PER-
sons, things of nature, and objects made by man. The
first are the most immediate—but in their bodily form they
have a painfully brief duration. The second are perennial:
they wear an air of primality. The third have the largest
popular appeal and are therefore the most questionable.
The chief example in this kind is of course the altar. Since
the beginnings of society the sacred slab or table with its
sacred food and fire has appealed more extensively than any
other symbol to the human heart. And like the motions of
the human heart the sacraments of the altar have ranged
the whole scale between brutal and sublime. Sharp revolts
and purgings, therefore, punctuate intense devotion in the
story of the altar.

Glancing over that amazing story, many excellent persons, during the past two centuries, decided that it was
drawing to a close, that reason and a purer religious sense
would presently abolish the altar. Doubtless the same opinion was held in India by many excellent persons more than
two thousand years before, when the Buddhist movement
was in its prime. But the art of perpetuating words was
then very far from its prime. The enormous printed record
of our modern revolt from the altar is lacking for earlier
occasions. We have to put up with the loss of the multitu-

dinous utterances of the average enlightened ancient Hindu. But we know that his situation, four or five centuries before Christ, must have had much in common with that of his occidental successor of the eighteenth century after Christ. Behind him lay a long, long era of the altar—an era that, taking its rise from the inspirations of holy men in a simple state of society, had become more and more involved in scholastic theories, mythic fancies, and elaborate practices. An outgrowth of "protestant" sects (as in the seventeenth century) had clumsily prepared the path of light; which, however, could be really followed only by persons who could free themselves utterly from the bonds of the altar. Such (as in the case of our eighteenth-century Enlightenment) must have been the common opinion of "enlightened" Hindus.

The Buddhist revulsion from the gods of the altar is supremely significant. Occurring in the very heart of Asia it was something between, and above, two other reforming movements belonging to the same great period of religious history, one to the east of it and one to the west. It surpassed Confucianism in religious intensity; it surpassed the Hebrew prophets in philosophic and ethical reach. As for our modern reformation—viewed as a single spiritual and mental process, within and without the pale of the Roman Catholic Church, rising in the close of the Middle Ages and still going on—certainly it is extraordinary for dramatic energy and range. But so far it has lacked a Buddha. Instead it has had, first, the late and narrow medieval mystics, then Copernicus, Luther, Erasmus, Calvin, Loyola, Descartes, and then—the successors of all those. Even St. Thomas Aquinas, if we accept the view of recent scholars who regard him as the protagonist of the modern movement rather than as the consummation of the medieval, cannot fill the vacant role. Sublime among scholastics, he is too scholastic for a Buddha.

The Enlightened One is unique indeed in the history of human enlightenment. More than any other he took up into his life and thought the spiritual meaning of the altar while abandoning the physical symbol. Sacrifice and justice, new vigor, joy, and mercy—he lived them and he taught them. His "supernatural generosity," to use a superb Hindu phrase, shone upon the needs of the common people around him. For them he condoned and indicated easier paths than his own. He himself, whatever may have been the attitude of the average enlightened man of his time, did not attack the altar. But he showed the way for future mankind, the only true and effectual way, to transcend the altar and leave it behind—*if* such be human destiny.

That destiny and that way, according to a common type of Christian argument, are entirely discredited by the so-called failure of Buddhism, capped by the high irony of Gautama's transformation to a chief god of the altar. But the argument on the other side also appears cogent. It may be condensed as follows: Unless a seed die it cannot have a new and greater life. Classic Buddhism had to go underground in order to be freed from its local and temporal shell and also because the world was not yet ready for it. The young peoples of the West had to have their own era of mythological imagination, pagan and then Christian, wherein their greatest prophet, Jesus of Nazareth, was transformed, like the Buddha, into a god of the altar. But that era is now closing, slowly and painfully. The unmistakable reaction taking place at present in favor of the altar is a ripple in a sinking wave. Far more significant is the steadily rising infiltration of the religious wisdom of the ancient East into the western wind. Unlike Christianity, that wisdom is in fundamental harmony with the findings of modern science and, more importantly, with the essential teachings of Jesus. The Buddha, freed from the Buddhists, can free Christ from the Christians. The ways of those two supreme teachers converge upon the spiritual highroad that stretches ahead of us, beyond the myths and cults of the altar. So this argument runs.

§2

Just here, however, one must remember that whether or not man abandons the altar he cannot abolish the class of objects in which it is comprised, any more than he can abolish the other two symbolic kinds mentioned at the beginning. Those two kinds, so long as they continue, will continue to produce the third. Since persons and the things of nature are symbolic, they cannot conjoin fruitfully without instilling that character into the offspring of their union. Persons, in the very act of winning from nature food and shelter and comfort, must create symbolic objects. Secular and religious purposes—taking the word "religious" in its most inclusive sense—are found indissolubly fused in the works of the earliest and latest men.

One of the best of recent buildings is the Post Office at Palermo, constructed in the spirit of the present Italian government. Its lines are massive and elemental. However, not far from its Doric portico you catch the motorbus that carries you out to the Doric temple of Diana at Segesta—also massive and elemental, but now with wind and rain, and dogs, playing among its columns. . . . No local cult can be so enduring as its adherents feel it to be. But it may embody something that is really elemental and permanent. The civic cult of Diana and its present successor in Italy, the national cult of Fascism, are both derivative from the old tribal religion of Productivity. Diana is one of the many forms assumed by the fruitful Mother Goddess who was worshiped in archaic times, with practices gross in the main but often rising to noble; as she is worshiped today, and will ever be, so long as man and nature continue. The raptive energy of Diana was no more essential for ancient hunting tribes than it is for modern tribes engaged in competitive industry; and it could not have been more ardently adored of old than now. Her wide-ranging fleetness of foot reappears in our vast electric maze of communications. And the modern post office, with its air-mail sanctuary, is a proper temple of Diana. On returning from lonely Segesta (of course with certain regrets) to the busy postal shrine of Fascism in the heart of Palermo, you may read, in imagination, above its grand portico an inscriptive verse from Swinburne's ode to the ancient goddess: "Over the splendour and speed of thy feet!"

In the courtyard of that building there is a huge stone figure of a soldier dead for his country, done in a style reminiscent of Babylonian gods; and above it towers in red marble the emblem known as the fasces. A building, a figure, a sheer emblem—these denote the chief modes of the sacred man-made object; and the modern age is extraordinary in its quantitative production of all three of them. The German Museum in Munich, housing a vast collection of tools and machines, is a temple of modern emblems. And one observes that the gay wonder in the faces of passing sightseers deepens often enough to reverence and even to awe, awe for the supernatural inventiveness of the modern mind. Which has its culmination, surely, in the moving and talking picture. Most of our other mechanisms, however important today, are liable to be discarded, or altered beyond recognition, when new scientific and industrial conceptions are brought forth by time. But time itself is brought forth by the cinema; it is the perfection of the old clock with figures coming out to act the hours. The film was latent in the art of the caveman, and its glimmering mimicry will go on so long as the reel of time runs. It gives a new turn and impetus to the religious symbolism of the human form. Henceforth the moving looks and tones of revered persons need not fade entirely from our screen of life. Suppose the cinema had been invented in ancient times: I fancy that even the modern thinker who, contemning symbols, wants to rebuild the spiritual life upon the distilled ideas of the saints and sages—distilled into human language, that great but imperfect symbol—even he, no doubt, would be tempted to visit a moving-picture temple wherein Gautama and Jesus were shown in their habit as they lived.

Personality, however, is never adequately bodied forth by its earthly forms. Admirers of a great man pass from one of his portraits to another, not satisfied by any and nonplussed by the ensemble. And the vivid ensemble provided by the moving picture is achieved at the expense of the selective art of portrait painters. Like the electron, personality cannot be fully caught when in motion, whereas if made to sit for its portrait it loses its moving existence. The dilemma is primordial and our perception of it is revivified by the cinema. When this invention was still new it was carried by an enterprising showman to a remote Maine countryside. He assumed that his audiences, cut off from the great world and thirsty for a sight of its leading figures, would be enthusiastic for "newsreels." But he soon found (so he told me) that he stood in danger of a "turnip-shower" until he consented "to feature screen-romances." The history of the cinema, that product of modern actual-

ism, is an extraordinary testimony to our yearning for ro-
mance; and this yearning is the effervescence of a deep human craving for that which is typical and lasting—for that
which is *superpersonal* if the word "person," so vitally ambiguous, is confined to its denotation of an actual human
figure. An actual moving picture of Jesus himself, perfect
in tone and color and in that final film-dimension which
now seems imminent, stereoscopic illusion, would soon become of secondary public interest. It would stimulate the
production of a series of screen-romances based upon his
life; and it would subside in their favor; and their favor,
too, would presently subside. . . . He said, "They would
not listen if one came to them from the dead"; and again,
"It is expedient that I go away from you. . . ." At our best
we acquiesce in the divine expediency of the transience of
persons. The nobler a person is, the more he reveals the inadequacy of his earthly form. In sublime moments he is
transfigured in the eyes of his close associates; and that intimate glory could not appear in the greatest conceivable
picture of him.

In a crowded cemetery near Florence the saddest objects
of all are the photographs of the departed displayed upon
their graves. One looks away to the springtime hills, "over-
smoked" (as Browning saw them) "with faint grey olive-
trees." We lift up our eyes to the hills when personal me-
morials press upon us blatantly; we seek in nature purer
intimations of immortality. Our modern nature worship is
largely a reaction from popular Christian personalism, Catholic and Protestant. Certainly at its height, a hundred years
ago, it brought a fresh and beautiful revelation of nature.
But in so far as it tried to satisfy the religious sense entirely
with so-called "natural" symbols, it was a clear failure. Today, by way of sequel, science has literally dismounted the

highest star: the heavenly *bodies*, from of old the supreme
signs of permanence, are seen to share the evanescence of
"faint grey olive-trees." No doubt this discovery is not so
revolutionary as it now appears; the latest men, like the
earliest, will, in a way, worship the stars. But the fact remains that our greatest age of physical science, which, re-
versing Ptolemy, began by making the stars stand still, has
eventually resolved them into whorls of gas ranging unknown orbits with supernatural speed. This fact is an after-
illustration of Francis Thompson's theme: the Hound of
Heaven, while constantly driving us out to the things of
nature, hunts us away from them with relentless love whenever we try to abide with them religiously. Their air of
primality, always so alluring to souls tired of history, is thin
as the stuff of stars.

Nature incites man to "idolize" his own brief form, to
depict it in an impersonal, a primal and typical manner.
This attempt on its lowest level gives rise to a host of curious figures, very ancient, very modern, in which the human
body is freed from personality by emphatic brute features.
But art in its loftiest moments, as in the great age of Greece,
is religiously impelled to distinguish the human form from
and above all others. Greek statues announce that man is
made in God's image. But their fate, as religious symbols,
announces that God is not the image of man; that beauty is
not truth—which is a blunt way of saying that natural
beauty, in its necessary striving for completion, has to forget that its completeness is necessarily incomplete. Therefore the highest kind of idol is that in which the beauty of
the human form yields to supernatural meanings. The most
reverential statues of the modern soldier are nobly emblematic rather than humanly handsome. The bronze Buddha
in meditation is seated forever above the region of Olym-

pian marbles. The accomplished loveliness of Raphael loses
the divine joy and sorrow of the Primitives. And Michel-
angelo's statue of Christ as a beautiful Greek athlete easily
bearing his cross, is a revolting hybrid. Nevertheless the
religion of beauty is a child, as well as an enemy, of the
beauty of religion. And one's dislike of the emblematic distortion of the human form in the interests of religion (the
Buddha's impossible legs, for example) is religiously justi-
fiable. Here one recalls the invincible hatred of idols shown
by the Hebrew Jehovah, along with his warm approval of
other sorts of symbol. His attitude in this respect, occasioned by local circumstances, was certainly extreme, but it
is also significant. The upshot is that the idol, though always
of real importance in a catholic view of religion, cannot
hold the central place among religious symbols.

That place belongs to the sheer or pure emblem; which,
from the earliest burial mound to the latest national flag,
from Jacob's anointed pillow of stone to the most elaborate
altar structure, has demonstrated its special hold upon the
human spirit. The emblem (so to call it for the sake of brev-
ity) takes up into itself the powers of all other symbols
while escaping their limitations. Unlike the idol, it does not
come into necessary conflict with our natural sense of
beauty. Visible charm is confined to its narrowest dimen-
sions in the case of the emblem; while its invisible charm is
surpassing and mysterious. The emblem is free from what
Meredith called "the taint of personality"; but it is also free
from the taint of impersonality which (in spite of Meredith) is the religious defect of external nature. The emblem
is a sign set upon nature, or rather stamped out from nature,
by personality. It condenses the potencies of the natural
objects that man intermittently worships, trees, springs,
hills, stars; but it condenses them beneath personality. Walt

Whitman's "beautiful bunting, flag of stars," flaunting the wide American landscape, meant, above all, the unfolding of a shining brotherhood of persons. And the swastika, an ancient sign of solar vitality, takes on new life when adopted by a strong national and personal cult: the Germans in awarding to their present leader an exceptional measure of personal devotion have felt all the more constrained to lift above him and above themselves an old enduring emblem. Such is the way of the emblem. In order to be thoroughly natural and intensely personal, it has to be superpersonal.

§3

Man may be defined as a symbol-believing animal. Men sometimes claim that they believe in nothing; but they cannot avoid symbolizing, in one way or another, the nothing in which they believe. Symbols are innumerable. A significant love for some object or creature, a child, a friend, a chair, a factory, a golf stick, is necessary to every man. Some one thing more than other things is for him "the real thing"—which is an immense claim when one comes to think of it—and he tends to undervalue the reality of the other things that other men adore. When a man declares that an altar, or a fishing rod, or a flag is "just a mere symbol" he means that for him an electron, a horse, or the League of Nations is far more richly symbolical. He fails to reflect that in denying reality to other people's symbols he cuts the ground from under his own. For it must be that all symbols, or none, have access to reality.

That issue needs to be made clear-cut. A capable modern philosopher has asserted that the history of his subject demonstrates at least this: from the standpoint of metaphysics there can be no real communion between a real Eternal and a real Temporal. The opposite standpoint appears in the bold verse of an old poet: "Eternity, who yet was born and died." [1] Those two standpoints may each be presented and labeled in a thousand different ways; but always the one denies, and the other affirms, that eternal reality is expressed in temporal forms. The one means that symbolism is radically false, the other, that it is radically true; and there is no proper compromise between the two views. A popular modern compromise is that of the man who likes to declare, broad-mindedly, "I know very well that the symbols which I love and live by are merely forms of self-delusion." But this man knows not what he says. Reality is precisely that which we love and live by, in so far as we really love and live: a symbol, no matter how illusory or even delusory it may be, has either some hold on reality or no real hold upon us. Nor can that reality be experienced as a merely temporal thing by a symbol believer. Whatever his foolish tongue may utter from time to time, his whole being knows that his chosen symbol, in so far as he loves it and lives by it, is a meeting of time and eternity. This communion, which may or may not be approved by the history of metaphysics, is established by what may be termed the history of histories, namely the story of human symbols. Human history, unless it is all delusion, turns upon an everyday awful fact: Eternity is, and yet is born and dies.

Man knows eternity in a real though secondary fashion through the symbols of the tribe. The most powerful of gods after God himself is the old Jehovah; under many names and emblems, he ever commands the tribe to increase and multiply, and leads it forth to battle. Man's primal urge to material productivity, divine in its way but deadly when

[1] Phineas Fletcher, *The Locusts*, 1627.

turned to low personal ends, rises to religion in the service
of the tribe. An advance in the means of production at any
time in history is normally accompanied by an intensification
of the tribal or national spirit; which thereupon accelerates
its constant trend towards war, war open or undeclared, in
so far as it does not succumb to material satisfactions. We
cannot serve God and Mammon, but we can serve God and
Jehovah. And the passing horrors of war can never be so
horrible to man, in his heart of hearts, as the steady deadly
glare that he finds in the eyes of Mammon. Man's divine
lust for life, life unseen and durable, drives him on from the
service of Mammon, who cannot be other than death in
life, to the service of Jehovah, who can be life in death.

But Mammon, aided by his friend Belial, is potently seductive. Milton's account of the pair in *Paradise Lost* is a
great unconscious prophecy of the path of social imagination from his time to ours. Men became more and more
devoted to an alluring Dream—peace, plenty, and piety for
all, to be effected by a new co-operation of the tribes of the
earth, by extraordinary advances in the means of production, and by enlightened devotion to the solid and progressive god called Nature. This deity, however, was mainly
Mammon in disguise. And soon the cool sword of science
proceeded to cut away from it the support that science had
lent to it: the solid evolution of the universe conceived by
the nineteenth century, is now revolving ether. . . . Rational
peace, limitless plenty, "natural piety"—the Great War,
the Great Depression, the Great Secession of Nature! The
scope of our catastrophe, said to be undreamt of, is propor-
tionate with the scope of the antecedent Dream. The Dream
is a very old one. Again and again tribes or nations in various parts of the globe have tried to get along together
peacefully and prosperously in the service of Mammon,

Mammon more or less disguised; and always the result has been, either a steady degeneration, or a renewed vitality from the bitter cup of war. When the Dream grows to a world dream, as in modern times, the sequel is a world tragedy—a vast demonstration of the fact that Mammon is a great god, that Jehovah is a greater, and that in human society Mammon is not subduable without the aid of Jehovah.

But Jehovah himself is subduable, since with God all things are possible. The Hebrew-Christian experience of the tribal god is the supreme episode in the history of symbols; it indicates the main plot of the whole human drama. It means that the tribe or nation is always the chosen people, always the main preliminary mode in which human society communes with the Eternal. The trials of the ancient Hebrews were select but thoroughly typical. Surrounded (like the modern Germans) by opposing tribes, they were impelled to worship intensely their own tribal spirit. It led them to develop their material life religiously, to fill efficiently and, at need, to forsake the fleshpots. It led them into struggles, brutal enough, with other nations. But also it enabled them at their best to discover the God of all nations, the Eternal at work in all of human history. They left as legacy to the Christian Church the conviction that Jehovah is an appointed ruler to whom must be given that which is due to Cæsar, but who by the grace of God may be subdued and lifted to the service of catholic ends. It was a devoted member of the most devoted of tribes who uttered and lived, beyond any other, universal words; as, Be ye perfect in charity as your Father is perfect.

In sacrificial devotion to his tribe a man learns that Eternity is born and dies, that universal Being is also personal and local. The familiar type of modern man who says that

for him the Divine Life, being everywhere, is never confined to places, would confine that Life to the place called
"everywhere"; which, for his children at least, is likely to
mean nowhere. This man is either a sadly tribeless person,
never finding Reality in one place more than another—a
home, a hill,[2] a factory, a capitol, according to the kind of
tribe; or, more probably, he does not really mean what he
says. Through the national tribe, through Jehovah, man
knows intensely that deity is more human, as well as more
divine, than man; that, because man is not everywhere, God
is where man most devoutly is. The courage and loyalty
developed by the tribe are essential elements of the justice
and charity adored by man at his best—adored, not as abstract virtues, but as revelations of a Life which is at once,
and so mysteriously, personal and superpersonal, working
through human places and emblems.

The chief place and emblem of that Life can be no other
than the altar. The tribal altar is properly the step before
the catholic (i.e., universal) altar. People speak bitterly of
nationalism "invading" the Christian Church. But true patriotism, at least, cannot invade the Church any more than
a person can invade his own home, if he is sane and sober.
Certainly the situation is tragic when a frenzied nationalism
is worshiped in a Christian sanctuary. But more significant
is the fact that the most intensely national of all the ancient
altars was the one that could best be transfigured to the
altar of the universal Christ.

Man must ever labor to build great nations and to build
above them a universal church. That twofold task, a magnificent challenge to the sacrificial powers of man (and of
God), may be rejected of men but it cannot be simplified.

[2] Perennial favorite site for sacramental meals of sun-worshiping
tribes, including our modern excursion clubs and nature-study groups.

To accept Christianity, in its catholic meaning, is to accept nationality. There is no vital alternative. One may despair, as some have done, of the whole of Western civilization. Or one may reject Christianity in favor of "vital" nationalism, as some are doing openly and as many are doing so obscurely that they know not what they do. But this too, in the long run, is the way of death and despair—not because it means war but because it means the refusal of the great life-giving twofold task that is laid upon human society. It means, in effect, the stultification of that very nationalism which it intends to glorify. For man yearns up through his tribes towards a glory that is higher. The cynic (this term means, not a person devoid of belief, but one whose belief in symbols is shallow and distorted) exclaims that in the World War the unreal God disappeared beneath the real gods of the tribes. But in fact, above those real gods the most real God reappeared. Always when men sacrifice supremely to Jehovah they recognize through him a greater than Jehovah; though as soon as the everyday world resumes its sway, the recognition begins to fade. But it cannot fade from the altar: it constitutes the altar.

This is the sole emblem that can never be either merely tribal or mistily universal. No wonder it is often hated by rabid nationalists, and despised by the followers of what I have called the Dream. Worse than despite, however, is the perverting patronage which those two opposite sects during the modern era have bestowed upon the altar. But all of this is testimony to the centrality of its position. Its enemies, whether attacking or despising or cajoling, must range themselves on opposite sides of that which holds the middle way, the highway, of human history. This situation was progressively obscured during the past four centuries by schism, "enlightenment," and dream, till the thunder of the

Great War clarified the air. At present the position of the altar is every day becoming more austerely clear. Certainly the Western nations are a chosen, an awfully chosen, people. They were chosen to carry tribalism to its ultimate development, material and religious. They have carried their industrial and scientific machinery to the ends of the earth; but first, they carried their Cross. This sign, placed by them upon the world's altar, became incorporate with it, lifting and pointing its perennial meaning. And this sign gives the meaning of the signs of the times today. Owing to Western vitality the world is now dominated as it never was before by the signs and emblems of productive nationalism; and the only emblem rising clearly above these, yet among them and able to sanctify them, is the Cross-crowned altar.

§4

The current movement towards the altar is therefore of central importance. But this consideration does not justify the conventional Christian attitude, noted above, towards the way of the Buddha. The significant fact remains that the man who next to Jesus has been most adored of men withdrew himself from the altar. This fact signifies that the greatest of emblems is also the most questionable, always in danger of deadly perversions, always in need of criticism and purification. Witness the amount of nonsense accompanying the modern Eucharistic revival. Doubtless superstition maintains a fairly constant level throughout the whole history of the symbol-believing animal, man; and modern superstitiousness, insidiously powerful because of its passing devotion to Nature and Enlightenment, may presently turn its current towards the altar, flooding it in a way worse than Elijah's way. Hence the Way of Abstraction, so to call the attitude carried to its height by the Buddha, is a continual and, in particular, a modern necessity. Known and used by Christ himself, it needs to be far better known and used by the Christian Church. The Way of Abstraction must be fully recognized by a catholic believer; but it must be recognized as, by itself, uncatholic.

For the meaning of the altar, not to say its power, cannot be extracted and abstracted from the altar. Every visible symbol, a person, a thing of nature, or an object made by man, has a whole meaning, or rather *is* a whole meaning, comprising what we call its spiritual and material meanings. This is because God himself, in whom all symbols live and move and have their being, is at once an inward and an outward life. That the outward aspect of a symbol ought, as men say, to be "kept in its right place," is a truism testifying that this place, however subordinate, is essential. To say, "I can do without such and such a symbol because I know what it really means," is a euphemistic way of saying, "I am willing to do without its real, full meaning." This meaning does not come away like the kernel of a nut; such a simile is a false image, an image against the truth of images. A nut is cracked and eaten and the shell tossed aside when the nut is a commodity, but not when it is a living symbol. A mere and sheer commodity—if such a thing could be—is a dried and cracked symbol. A symbol is a commodity's whole meaning and being as a fruit on the tree of life.

In loving a symbol and living by it—not in talking about it—one sees it, however dimly, as a living whole. One regards it, not just as a way of expressing a meaning, but as the way of knowing the meaning there expressed. We do not first find a truth that is vital to us and then look around for an object in which to embody it—a person, a tree, or perchance a family tree. We learn that truth, too well for words, in the symbol that we reverence. Man did not first discover the highest and fullest meaning of food, fire, and light, and afterwards invent the altar to emblematize that meaning. That meaning was, and is, discovered to him in the altar, discovered as inherent in divine humility and grace. The spiritual is recognized in and through the material; these two aspects of the Universe are known to be *at one* through sacrifice involving not just one but both. . . . This mystery, however, cannot be put into words. Otherwise the Word would not have made things, would not have become flesh, as the writer of the opening passage of St. John tries to express the matter in sublime inadequate words. But the mystery is more or less apprehended by every symbol-lover; that is, by Everyman. The meaning of the altar, like that of every great symbol, is a living whole, at once material and spiritual.

The case of Buddha shows how nobly a man may live upon the abstraction which we call "the altar's spiritual meaning." But it shows, too, how inadequate is that way of life compared with the Way, the Truth, and the Life. The parallel cited above between the Buddha and the Christ, drawn by those who wish to merge the meanings of the two, is an historical and a religious error—as grave as the error of those who deny all divinity to the Buddha. Through Buddha, God criticizes the story of the altar, criticizes it extremely because of extreme abuses. Through Christ, God enters into the story of the altar with a unique fullness of presence, lifting and establishing it. The life of Gautama was sacrificially spiritual. The life of Jesus was a complete religious sacrament.[3]

[3] This paragraph is in line with the Christological opinions expressed in the second half of the essay on Paul E. More, above.

Hence it opened the way for a true and progressive understanding of the physical aspect of life. Classic Buddhism, though free from the passing miraculous features of Christianity, cannot properly be said to be in fundamental harmony with the findings of modern science unless these findings are not fundamental. The Buddhist Nirvana, no matter how modernly and richly it may be conceived, involves a fundamental departure from the realities of nature. The Buddha warned his disciples against speculation regarding the nature of the universe; but such speculation was latent in his claim that his way was central. This claim, also made by Christ, connotes a radiating network of universal relationships open to the searching of the speculative intellect. Such searching, the more it is controlled by catholic experience, establishes more and more the claim of Christ. Whereas the position of the Buddha is seen to be, so to speak, sublimely off-center; the rays of richest human experience, physical and spiritual, will not converge upon it. The Buddhistic way of thought projects a picture of the universe which can be a whole only by never being wholly true to life. It goes aside from the full meaning of food, fire, light, humility, and grace. It indeed admits the fact that all life is symbolic; but it misses the life that is in all symbols; it misses the fact that, unless every symbol is entirely void of reality, all symbols must be seen to arrange themselves in vistas leading to the altar.

The Way of Abstraction, then, is properly a byroad—the most important byroad alongside the religious highway of history. Popularly speaking, it is the detour occasioned by the fact that the highway, being human, is incessantly in a state of damage and repair. Better, it is the pathway that thoughtful persons must continually tread—and should constantly leave behind. It is the way of winning that vital detachment from symbols which enables us to know how essential symbols are. . . . But the way goes farther off, and comes farther home, than any excepting One can know. It leads to those unknown hills where Christ meditated and prayed in unknown loneliness, whence He returned to the temple, to the cleansing of the temple, and to the sacramental meal through which He knew He would be known.

Index

Index